School Essays Letters and Phrases

Published by :
Lotus Press Publishers & Distributors

School Essays Letters and Phrases

A.K. Pillai

Lotus
PRESS

4735/22, Prakash Deep Building
Ansari Road, Darya Ganj,
New Delhi - 110002

Lotus Press : Publishers & Distributors
Unit No. 220, 2nd Floor, 4735/22, Prakash Deep Building,
Ansari Road, Darya Ganj, New Delhi- 110002
Ph.: 41325510, 23280047, 98118-38000
• E-mail : lotuspress1984@gmail.com
www.lotuspress.co.in

School Essays, Letters and Phrases

ISBN: 81-89093-98-3

Printed & Published by : **Lotus Press Publisher & Distributors,** New Delhi-02

Contents

PART - II — LETTERS

PART - III — PHRASES

Preface

An essay is a spontaneous flow of words that help to communicate one's ideas to others. An effective and well-written essay leaves a lasting impression on the reader.

Communication technology has greatly benefited mankind. The written word, denied for posterity, provides information for future reference.

An essay can have many purposes, but the basic structure is the same, no matter what. You may be writing an essay to argue for a particular point of view, or to explain the steps necessary to complete a task. Either way, your essay will have the same basic format.

If you follow a few simple steps, you will be responsible only for supplying ideas, which are the important part of the essay anyway.

Don't let the thought of putting pen to paper daunt you. This book explains the basics of writing essay and letters, supplemented by useful examples, and how you can use the common phrases in your communication.

ESSAYS

1. Essay Writing: The Basics

Every essay has to be written with the idea of communicating your thoughts in an orderly and clear manner. The following simple steps will guide you through the essay writing process.

First of all, decide on the topic that you want to write about. Then, follow the points stated below for drafting your essay:

1. Prepare an outline or diagram of your ideas.
2. Write your thesis statement.
3. Write the body.
4. Write the introduction.
5. Write the conclusion.
6. Add the finishing touches.

If you have already been assigned a topic, you still may not be ready to jump to the next step.

Think about the type of paper you are expected to produce. Should it be a general overview, or a specific analysis of the topic? If it should be an overview, then you are probably ready to move to the next step. If it should be a specific analysis, make sure your topic is fairly specific. If it is too general, you must choose a narrower subtopic to discuss.

For example, the topic 'Switzerland' is a general one. If your objective is to write an overview, this topic is suitable. If your objective is to write a specific analysis, this topic is too general. You must narrow it to something like 'Skiing in Switzerland' or the 'Scenic Beauty of Switzerland'.

Once you have determined that your topic will be suitable, you can move on. Organise your ideas. The purpose of an outline or diagram is to put your ideas about the topic on paper, in a moderately organised format. The structure you create here may still change before the essay is complete, so don't agonise over this.

Decide whether you prefer the cut-and-dried structure of an outline or a more flowing structure. If you start one or the other, and decide it is not working for you, you can always switch later.

Outline of Your Ideas

1. Begin your diagram with a circle or a horizontal line or whatever shape you prefer in the middle of the page. (see next page)
2. Inside the shape or on the line, write your topic.
3. From your centre shape or line, draw three or four lines out into the page. Be sure to spread them out.
4. At the end of each of these lines, draw another circle or horizontal line or whatever you drew in the centre of the page.
5. In each circle or on each line, write the main ideas that you have about your topic, or the main points that you want to make.
   a. If you are trying to persuade, you want to write your best arguments.
   b. If you are trying to explain a process, you want to write the steps that should be followed. You will probably need to group these into categories. If you have trouble grouping the steps into categories, try using Beginning, Middle and End.
   c. If you are trying to inform, you want to write the major categories into which your information can be divided.
6. From each of your main ideas, draw three or four lines out into the page.
7. At the end of these lines, draw another circle or horizontal line or whatever you drew in the centre of the page.

In each shape (or line), write the facts or information that support that main idea. Compose a thesis statement.

Thesis Statement:

Now that you have decided, at least tentatively, what information you plan to present in your essay, you are ready to write your thesis statement.

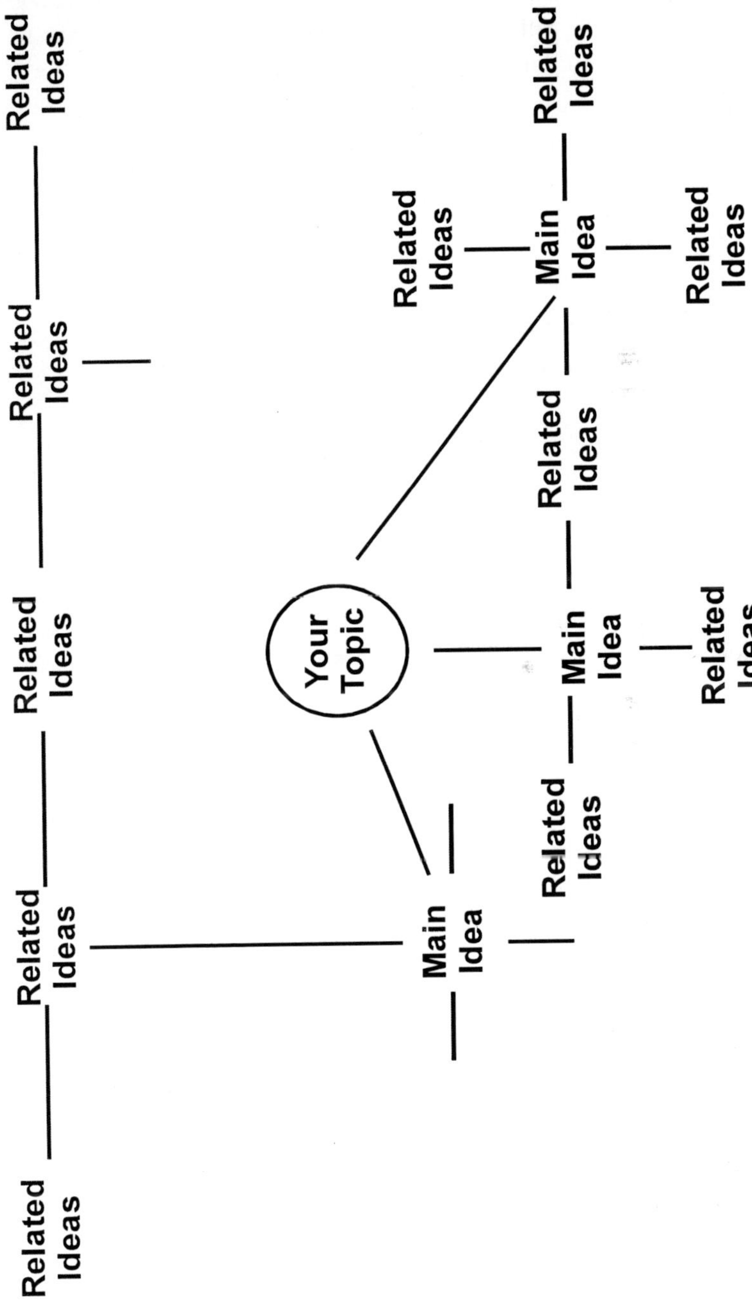
Your Topic
Main Idea
Main Idea
Main Idea
Related Ideas
Related Ideas
Related Ideas
Related Ideas
Related Ideas
Related Ideas
Related Ideas
Related Ideas
Related Ideas
Related Ideas
Related Ideas

The thesis statement tells the reader what the essay will be about, and what point you will be making. You know what the essay will be about. That was your topic.

Your thesis statement will have two parts:

1. The first states the topic:
   a. Switzerland's Scenic Beauty
   b. Building a Model Train Set
   c. Public Transportation.

The second part states the point of the essay.

a. Attracts travellers from all over the world.
b. Takes time and practice.
c. Can solve some of the city's most persisting and pressing problems.

Once you have formulated a thesis statement that fits this pattern and with which you are comfortable, you are ready to continue.

The Body Paragraphs

In the body of the essay, all the preparation up to this point comes to fruition. The topic you have chosen must now be explained, described or argued.

Each main idea that you wrote down in your diagram or outline will become one of the body paragraphs. If you had three or four main ideas, you have will have three or four body paragraphs.

Each body paragraph will have the same basic structure.

1. Start by writing down one of your main ideas in sentence form. If your idea is "reduces freeway congestion", you might say this: Public transportation reduces freeway congestion.
2. Next, write down each of your supporting points for the main idea, but leave four or five lines in between the points.
3. In the space under each point, write down some elaboration for that point. Elaboration can be further description or explanation or discussion.

   a. Starting point

   Commuters appreciate the cost savings of taking public transportation rather than driving.

b. Elaboration

Less driving time means less maintenance expense, such as oil charges, of course, less driving time means savings on petrol as well. In many cases, these savings amount to more than the cost of riding public transportation.

4. If you wish, include a summary sentence for each paragraph.

Introduction

The introduction should be designed to attract the reader's attention and give him an idea of the essay's focus.

1. Begin with an attention grabber. The attraction grabber you use is up to you, but here are some ideas:

   a. Startling information

   This information must be true and verifiable and it doesn't need to be totally new to your readers. It could simply be a pertinent fact that explicitly illustrates the point you wish to make. If you use a peace of startling information, follow it with a sentence or two of elaboration.

   b. Anecdote

   An anecdote is a story that illustrates a point. Be sure your anecdote is short, to the point, and relevant to your topic. This can be a very effective opener for your essay, but use it carefully.

   c. Dialogue

   An appropriate dialogue does not have to a identify the speakers, but the reader must understand the point you are trying to convey. Use only two or three exchanges between speakers to make your point. Follows the dialogue with a sentence or two of *elaboration*.

   d. Summary information

   A few sentences explaining your topic in general terms can lead the reader gently to your thesis.

2. If the attention grabber was only a sentence or two, add one or two sentences that will lead the reader from your opening to your thesis statement.

3. Finish the paragraph with your thesis statement.

Conclusion

The conclusion brings closure to the reader, summing up your points or providing a final perspective on your topic.

All the conclusion needs is three or four strong sentences which do not need to follow any set formula. Simply review the main points (being careful not to restate them exactly), or briefly describe your feelings about the topic. Even an *anecdote* can end your essay in a useful way.

The introduction and conclusion complete the paragraphs of your essay. Don't stop just yet. One more step remains before your essay in truly finished.

The Finishing Touches

You have now completed all the paragraphs of your essay. Before you consider this a finished product, however, you must give some strength to the formatting of your paper.

Look at your paragraphs. Which one is the strongest? You might want to start with the strongest paragraph, end with the second strongest, and put the weakest in the middle. Whatever order you decide on, be sure it makes sense. If your paper is describing a process, you will probably need to stick to the order in which the steps must be completed.

When you prepare the final draft, you must be sure to follow all the instructions you have been given:

a) Are your margins correct?

b) Have you titled it as directed?

c) What other information must you include?

Check your writing; nothing can substitute for revision of your work. By reviewing what you have done, you can improve weak points that otherwise would be missed. Read and reread your paper. Does it make logical sense? Do the sentences flow smoothly from one another? Are your spelling and grammar correct?

Once these small details have been looked into, your essay is ready for submission.

❖ ❖ ❖ ❖ ❖

2. Our President

Dr. A.P.J. Abdul Kalam is the eleventh President of India. He is India's best known scientist. He heads the mammoth Department of Defence, Research and Development.

Avul Pakir Jainulabdeen Abdul Kalam was born on October 15, 1931 at Dhanushkodi in Rameshwaram district, Tamil Nadu. His father had to rent boats to pay his school fee. He studied at the Schwartz High School in Ramanathapuram in Tamil Nadu.

After graduating in science from St. Joseph's College in Tiruchi, he enrolled for Aeronautical Engineering at the Madras Institute of Technology in 1954. He joined the Defence Research and Development Organisation (DRDO) in 1958 and served as a senior scientific assistant, heading a small team that developed a prototype hovercraft. But the project never took off. Following the lukewarm response to his hovercraft programme, Kalam moved out of DRDO and joined the Indian Space Research Organisation (ISRO) in 1962.

Kalam joined the satellite launch vehicle team at Thumba, near Thiruvananthapuram, and soon became the project director for SLV-3. He changed the very face of the country with his researches in space, building India's first satellite launcher, the SLV-3.

In the 1980's, he also made the country a missile power by developing the Agni and Prithvi, and was responsible for putting *Rohini* into orbit in July 1980.

Kalam returned to DRDO as its Director, and took charge of India's integrated guided missile development programme. The programme envisaged the launch of five major missiles.

In 1992, Dr. Kalam took over as the Scientific Advisor to the Union Defence Minister. Wearing a Gorkha hat in the Rajasthan deserts, he orchestrated India's underground nuclear tests at Pokhran on May 1, 1998, giving India weaponising nuclear capability. The scientist from a small hamlet in Tamil Nadu, who had dreamt of India as a nuclear power, many years ago, had finally achieved it!

In 2002, Dr. Abdul Kalam took over as the President of India. This humble son of a boatman, and a newspaper hawker himself in his childhood, hardly imagined that a day would come when he would lead a nation!

As a child, Abdul Kalam remembers being fascinated by the flight of seagulls. He has spent most of his life near the water frontiers of India. The newspaper boy of Rameshwaram coast on the Indian Ocean went on to the shores of the Bay of Bengal at Chandipur where he test launched missiles and checked on vehicles that re-enter the atmosphere from space.

Along the way to his degree in aeronautical engineering, and later to the supervision of the development of India's guided missiles, he found time to write Tamil poetry, and learned to play the veena. He refers to the *Bhagavad Gita* as often as he does to the *Quran*. It was from the *Gita* that he quoted to the reporters at Chennai after his nomination to the post of president of India was announced. When he is in Rameshwaram, he always makes it a point to visit the temple of Lord Ramanathaswamy. After being sworn in as the President on July 24, 2002, he quoted from Thivuvalluvar's *Thirukkural*, composed 2,000 years ago, to emphasize that for a nation to be prosperous, there should be no diseases, there should be high productivity, harmonious living and strong defence. The dreamer of the oceanic frontiers is also one of India's frontiersmen in technology – a technology that not only fired Agni and ignited the Prithvi, but one that can green the barren lands, provide food to the strong, and profit in world commerce. A First World dream that he dreams for a Third World nation.

It is a dream that he shares with Y. Sunderarajan, another technologist who had his stints in the ISRO. The duo are now dreaming up frontiers of technology-driven prosperity for one billion people. In this they are inspired as much by the grain-rich fields of the green revolution as by the success of remote-sensing satellites and re-entry vehicles. They see infinite energy that can be released not only from thermonuclear explosions but also from the human resource latent in the ordinary people of India.

In the book, *India 2020: A Vision for the New Millennium,* Dr Kalam and Sunderarajan identify exactly the bricks of technology that could build the dream.

Dr. Abdul Kalam lives a simple, spartan life in spite of receiving so many accolades in his life. In 1981, he was honoured with the Padma Bhushan, in 1990 with Padma Vibhushan, and in 1997 with Bharat Ratna, India's highest civilian award.

In his autobiography, *Wings of Fire,* he describes himself as a short boy with rather undistinguished borns, born to tall and handsome parents. In his race to success he has not left anything to fate. He says, "When one has orbited round the sun 70 times (he has crossed the age of 70) change becomes a necessity. This change must bring with it new thoughts which lead to innovative actions. I know my imagination will never let me down. Neither will my dreams. Technology can change the future of man. I have seen it happen in my lifetime." He also writes, "I will keep the lamp of knowledge burning to achieve the vision – Developed India."

❖ ❖ ❖ ❖ ❖

3. Walking Benefits

Walking is the safest and most convenient activity for weight control, ailment-free, healthy and all-round physical fitness. But walking also gives one a lot of pleasure and satisfaction. Walking is about success, growth, determination and deduction.

Did you know that walking uses large portions of muscle groups in your legs and arms in a steedy, rhythmic pattern? No wonder it is recommended for not just fitness but for total health too. It is the cornerstone of a total approach to personal fitness. Walking is one exercise that offers multiple advantages at a minimum cost and with least effort.

Walking increases the flow of oxygen to all tissues and cells. It increases the high-density lipoproteins (good cholesterol) which protects the heart and blood vessels from fatty deposits. It protects and strengthens the heart muscles whereby it can pump more blood with fewer beats.

Walking increases the ability of the body to handle stress successfully, making you less prone to blood pressure and heart disease. It decreases the sugar fats, known as triglycerides, thus preventing their being deposited on the lining of the arteries.

Walking also increases the efficient functioning of exercising muscles and blood circulation, so that muscles and blood can process oxygen more easily. It helps in increasing the number and size of blood vessels for better and more efficient blood circulation.

Walking favours more imaginative brain work by loosening the thinking process, and replacing straight line thinking by lateral and branched thinking, that is, delving deep into the mind. Walking is more conducive to web-like patterns of thinking.

Closely related to deep thinking is the sense of peace and calmness that comes with walking at a proper pace. A proper walking rhythm, coupled with the repeated contact with the earth, helps you to achieve this pace.

Walking for fitness will lead to health by better nutrition as well as exercise *per se*. By its very nature, walking is a safe sport, a moderate exercise that is easy on all the tissues of the bones, joints, muscles, tendons and ligaments.

A commitment to daily walking leads to an enjoyment of life that you may never have experienced before. It reduces tension, and provides a forum for relaxation and unwinding. It aids in problem solving and helps you to become mentally alert.

Walking is a positive way to handle anger, improve your disposition and point of view. It is a pleasant distraction from a humdrum life, and promotes a sense of general well-being.

Walking is non-competitive. It adds life to your years, and helps to develop a positive body image. It unclogs your mind, makes you self-reliant, and improves your posture.

Regular walking also sets the stage for meditation and spiritual progress. It has financial benefits to offer as well. Walk more whenever and wherever you can, thus saving on transport charges. Walking saves you money at the petrol pump, and in car repairs and maintenance. It cuts down on the need for prescribed drugs and on medical bills and hospitalisation costs.

Since walking is an exercise in itself, there is no need for you to join a formal exercise or weight control programme. Further, it does not necessarily need special equipment other than a pair of good and comfortable pair of shoes.

Brisk walking aids in sounder sleep, and promotes physical and mental health. It improves the skin tone and increases energy reserves, replacing fat muscles.

Remember, walking is the beacon of light in the fitness gloom. So walk whenever you can.

❖ ❖ ❖ ❖ ❖

4. A Visit to the Taj

An excursion into the past takes us to Agra to have a grand glimpse of the Taj Mahal, said to be one of the wonders of the world.

We boarded the early morning train to Agra from New Delhi railway station. It was a pleasant journey of three hours to Agra in the month of early November. We hired a taxi and reached the site of the Taj Mahal within minutes.

Oh, what a spectacular sight! This moment of Agra testifies to the perfection achieved by Mughal art in the seventeenth country.

We entered the site through the Taj Ganj gate which leads to the garden gateway. As you enter the huge red stone gate and stand on the platform, the whole panorama of the complex lies before you. The four exceptionally wide avenues cut by canals meet in the centre of the garden in a lotus pool.

Two symmetrical buildings in red sandstone with white marble domes a mosque and a guest hose — act as wings to the Taj Mahal, and leave behind them a terrace with a pavillion that overlooks the river Yamuna.

The Taj Mahal itself stands on a raised cubic structure with cut corners to give it the appearance of an octagon. The central building is crowned by a cupola which stands on a tall drum. Four minarets at the corners of the platform frame the magnificent mausoleum.

Huge entrances with bowl-shaped, highly decorated vaults lead through each of the four main tall facades. The beautiful ornamentation on the walls include panels with shoots of flowers in relief, scriptures from the *Quran*, inlaid with topaz, sapphire and other semi-precious stones.

Standing in the centre of the octagonal funeral chamber, connected by radiating corridors to the four entrances and four corner chambers are the cenotaphs of Mumtaz and Shahjahan, protected by marble lattices. Everything looks awesome and grand.

The use of Makrana marble that changes colour with the light gives the impression that the mausoleum emerges from the sky behind and almost floats on the green carpet of the garden like a romantic vision!

We sat on a bench and feasted our eyes on this glorious structure till we experienced a sense of serenity and satisfaction.

❖ ❖ ❖ ❖ ❖

5. Children and Television

In today's world of technological process, it is no wonder that many people find life more comfortable, yet more stressful. We find children and teenagers hooked on to the television for hours on end. This is a very sad state of affairs for everyone in general.

Television has a large impact on the attitudes, ideas and behaviour of children. Many of today's teens watch on television murders, rapes and heinous crimes perpetuated in the country. According to a survey, four out of five people are of the opinion that violence on television is a direct contributory factor to the way children view violence. They watch how these situations are handled and assume that this is how their life should be.

It behoves us, as parents, to instruct our children about the reality of television, what is shown on it is not reality, but something created to capture the interests of the viewers. In real life, such things hardly happen. You should be careful to see that your child is not exposed to the violent scenes on television, otherwise they will start believing that violence is the easiest way to settle conflicts.

Extensive television viewing promotes violence in many ways. These days, most working parents work round the clock to meet the demands of life, and have little time to spare for the children. The children are often left on their own in the house, and they spend their time watching television. Some programmes pose a lot of threat to them, as they are influenced by media violence without knowing it. They are too young to distinguish what is good or bad for themselves. Certain cartoon shows are depicted so realistically that children are likely to imitate what they see. Sometimes they leave a deep impact on the children's minds, as they have the ability to absorb what they see.

Most children are drawn towards the consumer culture. This leads to a change in their lifestyle. They find little time for social interaction. They get hooked on to certain programmes, and these become 'a must see' for them.

Television also exposes children to some positive aspects. Some of the educational programmes are worth watching. The Geographic Channel, the Discovery Channel and the History Channel have a lot to offer for a child's mental and educational progress. Quiz programmes are worth watching, very beneficial for enhancing their knowledge. Since all the members can watch such programmes together, this is an opportunity for the family to be together. A sense of bonhomie prevails, and knits the family into a close bond.

Parents must remember that children are influenced by what they are exposed to. So they must control what a child should watch on television. This will ensure that a child is positively influenced by watching television.

❖ ❖ ❖ ❖ ❖

6. The Value of Discipline

Discipline is the great binding force of a nation. It is the backbone of a nation. It is not something that is latent in a person, but something that has to be cultivated. It is a long process that starts from the family to society, from the society to the nation.

Discipline in a society and nation is necessary for the world to function smoothly and effectively. It is a valuable asset at all levels of society. Imagine a family or a school where indiscipline prevails. Children from such environments grow up being aggressive and ill-mannered.

Discipline involves people in doing their duty judiciously, diligently and sincerely. It is the essence of life, whose absence results in a nation beset with anarchy and restlessness. It is necessary in every walk of life and in every activity.

If there is discipline in schools, a child will learn to behave and follow the rules that are set by schools. It is a teacher's task in school, the parent's role at home, a manager's need in a company to inculcate the importance and sense of discipline in the citizens.

For most adults, discipline is a natural quality that comes naturally. They should set good examples for youngsters to emulate them. Children and teenagers are swayed by popular trends and styles which distract them from their path of higher progress. So they have to be disciplined to move on the right path. They therefore need guidance from elders, teachers and parents.

Discipline is born of a sense of responsibility among people. That is why European nations, and some Asian countries like Japan and Singapore, where you see a lot of discipline among their people, are so prosperous.

Our political leaders need to set good examples to their citizens, instead of being corrupt, haughty or indisciplined. All of us have witnessed their conduct in legislative assemblies and parliament, where they have resorted to throwing chairs and mikes. How can they expect the new generation to be better if they cannot set good standards for themselves? Only discipline can sustain a society or a nation. Discipline is the hallmark that distinguishes between progress and stagnation, success and failure.

❖ ❖ ❖ ❖ ❖

7. A Responsible Citizen

India is a nation with a rich cultural heritage of at least five thousand years. This culture sustains our nation, and the citizens of this nation sustain its culture.

All citizens of a country have certain responsibilities and duties which go hand in hand. Since India's independence, there has been a gradual decline in ethical and moral standards. This is because the focus has shifted from duties to the rights of citizens. People are now clamouring for their rights, and in the process, they are neglecting their duties as citizens of a nation.

All good citizens should shoulder their responsibilities. They must realise that they have to contribute to the prosperity of their nation, and not what the country can give them in return. Just as they sacrifice their time and efforts for their families, likewise, they should also spare their time and efforts in helping the country to move forward.

When elections come, the citizens cast their votes for the candidate who they think is honest and deserving. At such times, they should not think of casting their votes in the name of caste, creed or community. They have to exercise their freedom and rights in a proper and judicious manner.

As citizens of a nation, we must remember that it is our duty to remain faithful and do justice to our profession. As a doctor, treat all patients equally without any discrimination. As a teacher, see that all students get equal opportunity to prosper. As a social worker, ensure that the lower strata of people have access to higher education and jobs. As a government employee, take care of the common man and his problems. Provide the needy and the underprivileged with the basic needs of sustenance. As a lawyer, see that justice is done to the guilty and the non-guilty.

As a citizen of a proud nation, it behoves us to respect other people's ideas and opinions. Though each citizen has a freedom of speech, he must use it in a constructive way that provides results. But that does not mean he can have a verbal harangue with his neighbours or others. Have respect for the feelings of others, and guard what you say.

If you really care for your country which is teeming with illiterates, can you not spare half an every day to teach the rudiments of reading and writing to one illiterate person? It would indeed by a noble deed.

❖ ❖ ❖ ❖ ❖

8. A Journey in an Overcrowded Bus

In a country like India, where the population is very high and most of the people are poor, the bus in the cheapest form of transportation for long distances. Unfortunately, there are not enough buses to transport the masses from one destination to another. Hence, the buses are always overcrowded.

In a big city where distances are great, buses are normally overcrowded. You find children using the bus to travel to schools and colleges, men and women going to offices or shopping, patients going to hospitals, and so on. They are all jostling for a foothold in the bus. You find long queues at bus-stands, but when the bus arrives, everyone is rushing to get in, and the queue disappears.

I had a harrowing experience the other day. It was a hot summer day in the morning. I was waiting at the bus-stop to board the bus that would transport me to the spot where I was attending an interview for a job. I gave myself enough time to reach the place well in time to attend the interview, and some to spare.

After a wait of ten minutes I saw the bus approaching. I checked to see that I had the exact change to pay for my fare, and clutched my handbag tightly to my chest.

The bus stopped right in front of me with three others ahead of me. I waited for them to get in first as we were in a queue. But, wait a minute! Where was the queue? Before I knew I was nudged aside from someone behind me, and everyone was scrambling to get into the bus in a mad rush. I did finally get into it, but not before I had been pushed and shoved and stamped upon.

There was hardly any space to plant both my feet comfortably in the bus. The question of moving left or right, front or back was of course not there, as the bus was jam-packed. Being extremely hot and humid, I started sweating profusely. I could hardly lift my hand to wipe my face as there was no space – we were packed liked sardines!

After the bus stopped at the first junction, a few people alighted while some more boarded the bus. Every time the bus braked suddenly to a halt, I was nearly thrown off my feet, the only cold comfort being that the other passengers too were in the same plight. I had the misfortune to be right behind a woman who was stinking. It was quite an abnoxious odour emanating from her dirty clothes, but I was helpless.

At one stage, while the conductor was trying to weave his way through the crowd to collect the bus fare, someone's elbow dug into my rib cage, and I felt all my breath going out with a whoosh! I nearly fainted with pain, but fortunately, the pain soon subsided. I heard an exchange of heated words behind me. Probably someone else too had been hurt.

When I did finally alight at my destination, I felt like a sodden, filthy, sweat-covered ragged doll. But that was my fate. Fortunately, I had given myself enough time, and so managed to tidy up myself before braving myself to confront the interviewers.

I do feel sorry for those who have to face such problems every day!

❖ ❖ ❖ ❖ ❖

9. A Visit to an Exhibition

Exhibitions bring life to a city or town. There is a lot of activity, and people in large numbers troop in to see them.

Exhibitions can benefit in the form of imparting knowledge, sales of goods, a display of art or photography or stamps, and so on. There are exhibitions like slide shows, Railway Exhibition, Post and Telegraph Exhibition, International Exhibitions, Book Exhibitions, etc.

Last year, a grand exhibition was organised in our small town by the state government. This brought about a lot of excitement in the town. My friends and I decided to visit it one evening.

We found a long, serpentine crowd at the ticket counter. We fell in line and waited our turn. After purchasing our tickets, we entered the exhibition through a narrow gate.

Our first impression on entering the grounds was one of awe. It looked like a fairy land, lights glittered everywhere, and festoons decorated the arches and stalls. People were walking in all directions, and parents and elders held the hands of their children tightly so that they did not get separated from them. Generally, there was a lot of hustle and bustle around.

There were a number of stalls that sold various kinds of things. People in their splendid colourful clothes were seen moving from stall to stall, admiring or buying things that they desired.

As we approached the first stall, we saw a man dressed up like Humpty Dumpty, handing out sweets and candies to little children, some of whom clung to their parents in fear, while some of them were bold and curious enough to touch him. I was amused by the reaction of these tiny tots.

We passed stalls that sold clothes, books, household furniture, machinery, watches, plasticware, utensils, flowers (artificial), toys, household items, footwear, toiletry items, eatables and so on.

Finally we came to an open spacious area where a few stalls were set up to cater to the hungry folk. There was quite a spread to choose from – dosas and idlis, chana-bhaturas, knick-knacks, ice-creams, hot and cold drinks, Chinese fare, South Indian and North Indian delicacies, and various kinds of cakes, pastries and fried stuff.

Of course we were hungry, and so we sat down in the chairs that were provided for customers beside each stall.

While we ate our cakes and desserts, we noticed at some distance a man who was making his monkey do various tricks. Children were clapping their hands with delight. A small boy was trying to imitate the monkey.

We sat for a while enjoying the scenes around us. Finally we decided it was time to leave. We left the exhibition with contentment in our hearts.

❖ ❖ ❖ ❖ ❖

10. An Aeroplane Crash

Flying in an aeroplane is one of excitement and exhibiration. More and more people prefer to fly rather than to travel by a train or a bus, as it saves a lot of time. Businessmen are frequent travellers as also politicians and important government personnel and other dignitaries.

Now-a-days, we hear of frequent cases of planes crashes, both civilian and military. These occur in all countries, and the reasons for the crashes can be many. Whatever be the reasons, lives are lost, bringing despair to their families.

I had a harrowing experience during one of my travels by air to Delhi from Chennai. It was just that the Almighty took care of us, and snatched us from the jaws of death.

Our flight took off in the morning at the scheduled time. We all settled down in our allotted seats. The air-hostesses went about their jobs, attending to passenger's needs and generally ensuring that everyone was comfortable.

Before long there was an announcement that we were approaching Delhi. I looked out of the window and saw the scene way down below. Some buildings were discernible, and River Yamuna could be seen as a thin strip.

Just as I was sighing with relief that I would be on terra firma soon, I felt the plane shuddering. An announcement said that one of the engines had failed, and we may have to crashland. We were told to buckle our belts and to remain calm. There were fervent prayers, tearful eyes, shocked faces, fearful expressions. My heart was hammering away, and I silently prayed to my Lord to protect us all. The cabin crew went around pacifying the agitated. The 'No Smoking' signs came on.

The air-hostesses explained to the passengers the emergency exit procedures. We were told to bend our faces to our laps. Once the plane landed, we were to rush to the nearest exit and jump on to the inflated slides.

Soon we started losing height, the remaining engines screeching loudly. With the pilot controlling the descent and speed of the plane, we soon heard the loud thud of the wheels touching the tarmac. There were a few bumps, and then the plane stopped. We rushed to the exit as instructed, after loosening our seat belts, and jumped outside on the inflated slide that cushioned our fall. With our feet firmly on the ground we ran hastily towards the airport building as instructed by the cabin crew.

I turned just once as I ran, and saw smoke emanating from the front of the plane. I also saw fire engines rushing there to stop any outbreak of fire. Fortunately there was none.

Needless to tell, the crash landing of the aircraft left a fear in me. Since then I have not attempted to board a plane!

❖ ❖ ❖ ❖ ❖

11. The India of My Dreams

India is a country with a rich cultural heritage, but it is also the country with an exploding population and abject poverty. It is a country which has produced great leaders like Mahatma Gandhi, Rabindranath Tagore, Sir C.V. Raman, and so on, and can boast of greats like Mother Teresa, Annie Besant, to name a few.

Once known as the 'Golden Bird', India has been a home for many invaders like the British, the French and the Dutch, the Mughals, the Khiljis, etc. Our old civilisation, the vast knowledge in every field of life, and pearls of wisdom from the mouths of such saintly souls as Swami Vivekananda, Shankaracharya, Ramakrishna Paramahansa had endeared us to the outside world. Now, all that past glory, the golden eras have all vanished.

Today's India is ridden with strife, nepotism, corruption, terrorism, poverty and whatnot. There has been a general decline in the ethics and moral standards among its citizens. There is vast unrest between states squabbling over sharing of river waters, vast movement of population from the rural to the urban areas in search of lucrative jobs resulting in overcrowded cities, lack of civil amenities in most villages, lack of proper shelter and drinking water in many areas, and much more.

The India of my dreams is one where there is harmony and unity in diversity. Petty quarrels amongst states and politicians that can result in anarchy and social unrest must be arrested. People should have the freedom to travel unhindered from one end of the country to the other.

I would like to see every human being getting three square meals a day with good potable water, a shelter over his head and some job that could help him in his sustenance.

There should be good civic amenities, and a high standard of hygiene and sanitation. Roads should be well paved to facilitate better transport.

Educational institutions should aim to make all the citizens of India literate, whether old or young, women or men, blind or deaf. There should be compulsory education for all, at least till the primary level.

Population should also be an issue of focus. With better education and propaganda, the rise of population can be controlled, bringing about complementary benefits. With small family norms being stressed upon, opportunities for employment increase. Every person would have the pride of being employed according to his talents and capabilities.

With better sanitation and hygienic conditions, there would be lesser cases of health problems. Agriculture and industries should get a boost for better production and turnover, so that India is self-sufficient and never in want.

With the economic scene in India getting better, there is hope yet for India to be a leading nation. Air, noise, water, nuclear pollution being taken care of, India can positively march towards an era of prosperity, social harmony and non-discrimination.

❖ ❖ ❖ ❖ ❖

12. The Autobiography of a Rupee

I lie here in this corner of the small box, along with two buttons, an eraser, a few bits of paper, and small plastic beads. I have been here for over three years, neglected and weary.

There was once a time when I was gazed upon with awe and wonder. Today, I lie here with most of my face effaced, having lost all my shine and splendour.

I came out of the governemnt mint with my companions, all of us shining silver. Each of us had a lion's head, with the lettering clear and distinct. I felt very proud of my bearing!

I started active life when I was handed over the counter to a bank employee who dumped me with my colleagues in a collection box. I lay there for about three days. Then I was handed over to a shopkeeper who took me with my colleagues in exchange for a cheque, and kept in his wallet. On reaching the shop, he placed me in a till. He gazed at me for a while, admiring my shine, then closed the till.

I found myself surrounded by many similar coins, but of different sizes and different metals, different stages of erosion, with different years embossed on them. I felt like a king among them, and preened myself to that effect! There were a few like me, but older, and dull and worn – as I am today. One old coin advised me in kind words to always respect old rupees and keep the small change in their place, for a rupee is always a rupee, no matter how old.

Soon I found myself in a lady's handbag, but not for long. I was dropped in a telephone kiosk from where I went into a pretty house. I was handed over to a child who put me in a piggy bank where I lay with others for two months. Then I was handed over to a toy shop, an old man, a restaurant, a smart businessman, a beggar, a fruit vendor, a child who finally put me in the box where I am today. Now I lead a dull life, but I feel I now need this rest, for I am old.

❖ ❖ ❖ ❖ ❖

13. If I Win a Lottery

What a nice feeling to have if you know that you have won a lottery, and that soon you will have wealth at your disposal! Imagine what all you can do with such a bonus! Such a windfall to fall in your lap would be anyone's dream.

Well, if I win a lottery that assures me of great wealth, my first task would be to visit the temple of my deity, and offer my sincere thanks to the Almighty who endowed me with this blessing. I would donate generously to the temple so that they can feed the poor on an appointed date.

The next item on my agenda is to move into a small but comfortable house with modern amenities. Having came from a lower middle-income background trying to eke out a living with whatever is available, I would now like to relax and not worry much about where my next meal came from.

I have always dreamt of a small but neat and spacious garden which has a lawn and some beautiful perennials. I would see that a few trees are planted in the periphery of the garden.

Then I would like to invest the bulk of whatever remains wisely—not in shares but in savings schemes that have no risks whatsoever. I would ensure that I get a steady income every month. With a regular, satisfying income, I would now like to channel my services to the needy and underprivileged.

The first step towards helping the poor would be to visit the slum areas and see what can be done to improve the lot of the people living in below-poverty conditions. I would like to build 'pucca' two-room houses for at least most of them, and ensure that they have good drinking water and hygienic surroundings with proper sanitation. I would visit these areas personally to see that the people here are happy. It would be like adopting a colony for the betterment of society.

Next, I would like to see all the children in the area going to schools nearby while the uneducated elders attend basic courses in literacy in the afternoons before the children return home.

After all this, if I still have a substantial amount remaining, I would like to donate regularly to an orphanage nearby. It is such a joy to see the smiling faces in an orphanage where children are given so much love and attention, and who are completely at the mercy of others for their day-to-day living.

I am sure most people would like to spend their money in a useful way if they ever won a lottery. Well I hope so!

❖ ❖ ❖ ❖ ❖

14. Traditionalism Versus Modernlism

India, with a rich heritage of traditional and modern cultures, can take pride in its civilisational greatness. Some of its old traditions still prevail side by side with modern progress.

Old traditions give way to modern traditions. When these traditions too last for some time they are replaced by more modern ones; hence, all traditions are the result of modernism.

While traditions often bind and unite us, modernity generally keeps us apart from each other. Much of our old traditions are beliefs and customs that have been handed down to us by our ancestors. They have their roots in the past.

Our old traditions are steeped in rituals that bear no logic or religion, but are yet practised as traditional customary practices. You hear of the old practice of throwing a handful of rice over your shoulder, or a bride kicking a pot of rice on entering her new house after marriage. These are traditions that still prevail in most places.

But modernism is the mantra for the younger generation. There are very few in the younger generation who still follow old traditions. With the world progressing we cannot afford to be left behind with our traditional ways that may not suit the trend. But in the process of moving towards modernism we have to maintain a proper balance between the two.

Science and technology propel us towards development and better living conditions. We have to sift the good from the bad, and retain those traditions that are beneficial to us. This will help us to preserve our traditions as well as move forward towards future development of the country.

❖ ❖ ❖ ❖ ❖

15. The Importance of Leisure

In this fast-paced jet-aged world, people are so busy that they virtually have no time for leisure. The end result is a tension-filled life. Caught in the rat race of competition and money-making racket, it is very important for each one of us to find time for relaxation of at least an hour.

To escape the daily grind of routine work and the hassles of toiling throughout the day, leisure provides that opportunity for one to rest and relax. It gives you the time to enjoy the beauty of nature, have a chit chat with neighbours or relatives, make social calls, spend quality time with your near and dear ones, or just sit back and watch a television programme that provides some light comedy. This way you unwind from the pressures at your workplace.

There are various ways of spending your leisure hours. If you have a hobby, then engage yourself in it – light reading, stamp collection, picture postcard collection, photography, watching movies, social work, gardening, and so on.

If you are an avid reader, books or magazines can be entertaining as well as relaxing. You may come across something that interests you which can be stimulating for your mind.

Gardening is another hobby that brings a lot of joy and cheer to you, as you are close to nature. The riotous, profuse colours of flowers and plants are a delight to watch. The thrill of watching them grow and bloom brings immense satisfaction to anyone.

While stamp and picture postcard collection offers you a lot of information about other countries, photography allows you to be very creative. The experimentation with black and white, and colour photography can be a useful leisure activity. Capturing those special moments in time for posterity can be an exhilirating experience.

Letter-writing, cleaning cupboards, craft making, painting — these are other activities that can help you to relax. Or you can just go out for a walk and enjoy the beautiful sights that nature has to offer. This will surely provide solace and joy to the mind as well as the body. If you have young children at home, spend some time playing with them, for they too give you a lot of joy while they receive a lot of love and attention from you.

❖ ❖ ❖ ❖ ❖

16. Violence and Terrorism

While the whole world is engaged in its efforts to make this earth a peaceful world, ironically wars and disputes between country and country, and state and state, are escalating. With fast-paced progress and development of humanity towards modernity, there is side by side the growing trend of violence and terrorism.

Take, for instance, the terrorist attacks in Kashmir, in the USA, in Israel and Palestine, Russia, Pakistan, Afghanistan, Iraq, London, and so on. Human bombs have become the norm of the day. The threat of a nuclear war is ever looming large, and more and more countries are interested in arming themselves with this destructive nuclear arsenal.

Violence is committed in the name of patriotism or love for one's country or religion. What is at stake are the innumerable deaths that result due to the selfish motives of a few. These few are the fanatics who have the false misconception of avenging the heinous crimes committed by other fanatics. It is a vicious circle where man hates man, and a cut-throat game is played.

While some countries are genuinely moving heaven and earth to bury their differences and live in neighbourly peace, there are other social elements who are misguided in their commitment for their country by using violence as a means of retaliation.

Man can survive only through peace, harmony and comradeship. The peace process takes a long time for accomplishment, but it has to be initiated soon. This needs the involvement of all nations, and a lot of cooperation and give-and-take attitude of people by and large. Let us all get together and join hands to make this world a beautiful and happy place to live in.

❖ ❖ ❖ ❖ ❖

17. Rising Prices in India

Today, India is progressing towards becoming self-sufficient in many areas. But the main challenge facing its people is the unprecedented price rise of all important commodities. This has affected not only the living conditions of the people at large, but also the economic scenario in the nation.

Prices of foodgrains, sugar, petrol and diesel and medicines have escalated sharply. The common man is hard hit and finds it difficult to eke out a living. Such soaring prices necessitate more members in the family pitching in to earn some money. No wonder there are so many dropouts from schools in the lower income strata of people.

What India lacks is a good system of procurement and distribution. Increased agricultural production and industrial goods can arrest inflationary pressure and price rise. This is something that the present government needs to focus on.

With the price of petroleum products soaring globally, the Third World countries especially are finding it extremely difficult to keep pace with the others. This leads to poor countries becoming poorer, while the oil-rich countries are thriving and growing richer. Imagine the plight of the millions who cannot get even two square meals a day.

One doesn't feel the pinch if the costs of consumer or luxury goods rise, but if the prices of essential commodities rise, where does the common man go? Starvation and deaths are quite common in poor countries where so many people have no shelter, clothes or food.

In India, the government needs to ensure that foodgrains are distributed through fair shops without the middleman swallowing half of them. Government personnel should carry out sudden checks to ensure fair distribution of these goods reaching the common man for whom they are intended. Black marketers and hoarders should be nabbed and punished. Corruption should be wiped out and stringent measures must be employed for this. Only then can we hope to see economic benefits for the rural poor.

❖ ❖ ❖ ❖ ❖

18. Beggary in India

India is a poor country that is mostly constituted of villages. The teeming millions reside in the rural areas where some of the people live even without good pottable drinking water.

On the other hand, are the large cities that are bursting at their seams with urban population, where the infrastructure is unsuitable to give shelter to all its citizens. In the capital city of Delhi, or the congested city of Mumbai, slums keep mushrooming, for there is a general movement of the masses from the surrounding rural areas to these cities in search of jobs. Unable to find jobs, and nowhere to live, they resort to begging.

There is a general belief among foreigners visiting India that begging has been prevalent here for centuries. Not so. It started with the decline of cottage industries when the British ruled India. It was the time when the general poverty in India was at its worst. The British had the people working for them more or less as slaves, doing all the menial work for them. Very few Indians were in their top heirarchy. This is when begging set in as the destitute had to live on the charity of others, having no income or job of their own.

You can still see beggars in large cities where they live side by side with the rich. Their jhuggi-jhompris are getting legalised as the politicians seek votes from them. It is a pitiable sight that these hovels offer–dirty, unkempt, pot-holes, stugnating waters, lack of civic amenities, and so on.

The government has been hard-pressed to solve the problem of beggary in a practical way. Proper houses, better sanitation system, good and clean drinking water are the thrust areas that need to be focused on. The government should encourage them to work by offering them jobs in handicrafts industries. Even the handicapped can be given suitable jobs there. Cottage industries, handloom weaving, basket making, cane furniture industry can all make efforts to give them a foothold in their industries so that these beggars too can earn a decent living and live with dignity.

❖ ❖ ❖ ❖ ❖

19. The Evils of Corruption

Corruption is a form of evil that eats away the roots of an established civilisation, leading to anarchy and mismanagement at all levels of government. Right from the heads of bureaucracy to peons and fourth class workers corruption has become a way of life for them. Even an honest being is suspect if he happens to come into some wealth.

While corruption has not mushroomed suddenly, being existent right from the time of creation of human life, when Satan tempted Eve to the apple of knowledge, it has produced a chain effect of evil. As Machiavelli says in his *The Prince*, "If the chief party, whether it be the people, or the army, or the nobility, which, you think most useful and of most consequence to you for the conservation of your dignity, be corrupt, you must follow their humour and indulge them, and in that case honesty and virtue are pernicious."

We have heard of corruption being widespread in all countries. Consider the Watergate scandal, Bofors, Lockheed in Japan and so on. Politicians are caught on camera accepting bribes, and the police is not either spared. Governments come and go; wealth passes from hand to hand; politicians and bureaucrats become wealthy overnight; a below-average student gets admission in the best educational institution; an applicant for a prestigious job gets it through backdoor; etc. There is no place where corruption has not reached its tentacles.

The long arm of the law is unable to stem the root that has set in, for even the judges are not beyond corruption. How can the institution of justice thrive in such a field of corruption?

❖ ❖ ❖ ❖ ❖

20. India in 2010

India's strength lies in celebrating its diversity. Its plurality is not only in terms of religion but also in every other conceivable aspects: language, culture, habits, etc. In every field of activity, India is gradually making a progression towards self-sufficiency. We are witnessing several positive changes that will lead the nation into becoming a powerful and prosperous country by 2010. Unless there are some devastating natural calamities, India can hope to become another superpower.

Though we are expected to forge ahead on the population front, ahead of China, efforts are being taken to curb the population explosion in India. While China has adopted the one-child norm, India is still stuck with its two-child programme. Educating the rural poor is providing positive results and we hope to see a drastic check in population rise.

In information technology India has forged well ahead of many First World countries like China, Japan, France, Britain, etc. This has ensured a prominent place for India on the world map.

There has been tremendous increase in food production and self-sufficiency, so much so that we have started exporting foodgrains to other Third World countries. Armaments and other defence products are also earning national revenue through exports.

In the area of space exploration, India has a bright future. With the launching of Aryabhatta, Bhaskara I and II, India's remote sensing satellite, PSLV C 2 and GSLV, the Indian space programme has brought about a sea-change in our telecommunications, weather forecasts and other geographical studies and research.

By the year 2010, India is bound to have better transport facilities, housing, development of rural areas, safe drinking water for every citizen, better hygiene, health and sanitation conditions, and employment for every citizen of India.

❖ ❖ ❖ ❖ ❖

21. The Horrors of War

The past generation produced some great men but as a generation it led the world repeatedly to disaster. Two world wars are the price that has been paid for the lack of wisdom on man's part in this generation. It is a terrible price to pay. The tragedy is that, even after such a disastrous price, we have failed to purchase real peace or an end to conflict. An even deeper tragedy is that mankind does not profit by its experience, and continues to go the same way which led previously to disaster.

How can peace be preserved? Not by attacks or compromising with evil or injustice, but also not by talking and preparing for war. The process of dividing the world into two camps increases the conflict. It produces a sense of terrible fear in the minds of men.

A war is fought to gain certain aims. The defeat of the enemy is not by itself the aim but rather the removal of an obstruction. A case in point is the attack on Iraq by USA to remove Saddam Hussain.

War today has become an instrument of total annihilation of a whole society. The innocent children and women, who have no role in the wars, are sacrificed at the altar of wars. Senseless firing and bombardments leave a sea of destruction around.

Bombardment of civilian and residential areas lead to havoc and disaster in its wake. Homes are destroyed, people are separated, there is disruption of normal life, lives are lost, and so on.

It has also become commonplace to have ethnic conflicts, as in Sri Lanka where the Eelam Tigers want autonomy and their own land, the Bosnian Muslims in Serbia, the Palestinians in Israel, etc.

We are a member of the family of nations and have fully acceded to the obligations of the United Nations. We have to abide by these rules and ensure that there is everlasting peace in this strife-torn world.

❖ ❖ ❖ ❖ ❖

22. Atomic Energy

Atomic energy for peaceful purposes is what the world needs. The energy released from atoms when they are pulled apart, or when an atom breaks into two, is very powerful. Harnessing such energy for peaceful purposes can be extremely useful to mankind. The two atomic bombs dropped over the Japanese cities of Hiroshima and Nagasaki involved a lot of research before they could be utilised. This was used for a destructive purpose whereby there was untold misery and utter devastation in these twin cities. The aftermath of the bomb explosions left behind intolerable conditions for humankind. The Nagasaki type of bomb was a crude, conventional one, but its impact was very high, where many people fell prey to cancer and other dreaded diseases.

Today, countries all around the world are engaged in the deployment of this energy for useful purposes. One such use is to drive turbines that produce electricity that is both cheap and of very good quality. Power can thus be generated with the use of a very small amount of nuclear raw material.

Atomic power is also used in ships and submarines, as power for lighting up cities and towers, and for the use in domestic appliances. This also saves on consumption of coal, petroleum and wood as sources of energy.

Another very beneficial use to mankind is that atomic power can be harnessed for curing deadly and fatal diseases like cancer, tumour, etc. Hospitals and medical institutions find it useful in surgery and other diagnostic applications.

Scientists the world over are using atomic power for research in various fields of science. While rockets are being fuelled by nuclear power, space stations run on atomic power, neither being a threat to the atmosphere. Used judiciously, they are also non-toxic. Very little of the atomic energy is required for very large proceses. Hence, there is very little need to store it, and industrialists can therefore conserve space for other production units.

The positive gains from atomic energy far outweigh the negative aspects. Therefore, atomic energy should be used peacefully for the benefit of mankind.

❖ ❖ ❖ ❖ ❖

23. National Integration

Nationalism is the binding force that unites the people of the nation. This becomes clear when all the Indians united as a whole to oust the British from their sacred soil, their hallowed land. This was because of their commitment to knit together as one whole unit. This is what is national integration and unity.

The British in India adopted a policy of divide and rule, manipulating the Indians for their own selfish gains. They instigated religious intolerance among the Hindus and Muslims who had before lived together in harmony in brotherhood. This resulted in their division along the lines of caste, religion and language. India saw a rift in the relations amongst its people, where the Hindus and Muslims were pitted against each other. This led to the formation of Pakistan.

After independence, the scene is much the same. Christians too are being targetted in the process. People belonging to different religions are trying to have the upper hand. While the minorities still enjoy the benefits of a secular government, there are fanatics who would like India to be a Hinduistic society.

What India today needs is to once again strive for national integration. It is a secular nation where every Indian has the right to follow his own religion.

India is a country rich in its culture. It has several cultures, religions and languages. As George P. Morris says in his *The Flag of Our Union:*

The union of lakes – the union of lands –

The union of states none can sever –

The union of hearts – the union of hands –

And the flag of our union for ever!

It is very important, if India wants to go in the right direction of everlasting peace and progress, to be united. Very few Indians think of themselves as Indians first and Hindus, Muslims, Christians or Sikhs later. This attitude of not considering themselves as Indians first should not be encouraged.

Communals riots arc prcvalent in many pockets of India. Terrorism and Naxalite problems are threatening to break apart the nation. People clamouring for separate statehood, and disputes over sharing of river waters are not conducive to national integration.

It is our duty as Indians to sort out these trifling snags, and then march ahead towards progression. Let us be proud to be Indians first and preserve our Indian identity.

❖ ❖ ❖ ❖ ❖

24. Religious Tolerance

India is a secular country that boasts of various religious communities, like Hindus, Muslims, Christians, Sikhs, Buddhist, Jains, and so. The people of these communities all live together under of the umbrella of Indianness. Religious tolerance here is the backbone of its cultured and civilised society, as it is ingrained in the Indian psyche. As Arthur Helps puts it, "Tolerance is the only rest test of civilisation."

India has been a host to many religious establishments. Buddhism and Janism took their birth in this sacrosanct land. The Muslims invaded

India in waves, right from the time of Muhammad bin Qasim in AD 711 till the Mughals got a foothold here in the early sixteenth century. The Christians settled here after the arrival of St. Thomas in AD 52, who founded seven churches in Kerala. Swami Vivekananda remarked in the Parliament of Religious held in Chicago, "I am proud to belong to a nation which has sheltered the persecuted and the refugees of all religions and all nations of the earth."

It is religious tolerance that has cohered India into a single entity. It is the land where great nobles from all religions have lived together side by side in harmony, for whom the principle of first being Indian before being to a particular religion elong uppermost.

The running and uniting theme that binds all religions together in India is that there is one God, you may call Him by any name. As Vivekananda put it, quoting the *Gita*, "Whosoever comes to me, through whatsoever form, I reach him; all men are struggling through paths, which in the end lead to Me." Just like different streams have sources in different places, but finally all mingle their water in the sea, likewise all religions lead to the same goal – the Almighty God. Let us hope that India continues to remain secure, and nurture its religious tolerance attitude towards one and all.

❖ ❖ ❖ ❖ ❖

25. Dowry Menace

Dowry practice in India is a curse that has spread its poisonous tentacles to all corners of the country. It has not spared any caste or community. It is a shame that it is so prevalent in a society that has such a rich traditional culture.

Dowry system has been in practice in India since the ancient days. Girls and boys were married while they were hardly in their teens. The parents sent their daughter to her new home with lots of gifts and basic necessities that would sustain her and her husband till such time as the husband was old enough to start earning. This age-old tradition continues today, but now it is greed — that of the groom's folks — which has made it a social evil.

In this modern age, were girls are given equal opportunities for higher education and better jobs, parents are wary of giving away their daughters in marriage to someone who is lesser qualified than them. On the other hand, if the boy has a high social standing and status in society, and has a very lucrative job, then there is increasing demands made by his parents in the form of dowry. Many families cannot afford to meet these demands, and find their daughters left high and dry on the shelf. Late marriages, deaths and suicides, and bride-burning are a few commonplace occurrences, especially in North India.

The Indian government has constituted laws making the practice of accepting dowry illegal. But parents find loopholes in the laws and extract goods in various other ways in a subtle manner.

Girls and boys who enter into wedlock should take the initiative and put their foot down when the subject of dowry crops up. It is not enough for the girl alone to take a stand, the boy too should be firm with his parents and try to break the shackles. It is up to the government to wipe out this social menace from the face of its soil.

❖ ❖ ❖ ❖ ❖

26. Protection of Wildlife

The National Wildlife action plan adopted by the Indian government in 1983 provides the framework of strategy as well as programme for conservation of wildlife. But there is imminent danger of some endangered species disappearing altogether as there is unchecked poaching going on in several wildlife reserves. In spite of having diversified wildlife in abundance, the threat of their becoming extinct looms large.

The reasons for the depletion in the number of wildlife are many. One great cause is man's greed for money which makes him a compulsive poacher. Tiger skins, ivory tusks, hippo and elephant hides, snake skins, frogs, and so on are exported to the Far East for lucrative sums. Project Tiger has been in operation for over two decades, but the tigers are disappearing very quickly. The government has finally woken to the fact that illegal poaching has been going on unchecked. If official reports are anything to go by, in nearly 15 years, an estimated 1,500 to 4,500 tigers have been killed by poachers, and exported to China, Taiwan, Hong Kong and Vietnam. Their skins, claws and other parts are used as show pieces and for medicinal purposes.

The rhinoceros from the Manas and Kaziranga Wildlife Parks are killed for their matted horns and hides. Leopards are killed and exported to Russia and East Europe. The musk deer in the Himalayan regions provide the musk perfume, catering to the European market demands for their cosmetic industry.

The black bears are slaughtered for their gall bladders that are used in Chinese medicines, snakes for the skin that is turned into belts and purses, mongoose for their bristly hair for making brushes.

Under Project Elephant, financial, technical and scientific assistance are provided to states having free-ranging population of wild elephants. Drastic measures must be taken to curb poaching. The need of the hour is to equip anti-poaching staff with arms and mobile phones, who can be depended upon to nab the offenders. The people of the surrounding areas of these reserves too should be educated to protect the animals that might wander into the village.

❖ ❖ ❖ ❖ ❖

27. Nuclear India

With the underground testing of three nuclear devices in May 1998, codenamed 'Operation Shakti', India became the sixth nuclear weapon power in the world. India became a nuclear weapon-capable power way back in 1974, when it conducted the first underground test at Pokhran range in Rajasthan. It was a demonstration of India's nuclear capability, coupled with a political statement that India would not make the weapon unless threatened.

With the tests, India attempted a change in the world order, dominated by five nuclear powers – the USA, Russia, China, the UK and France – all permanent members of the UN Security Council. They dissuaded North Korea from making the bomb, cajoled Pakistan to give up its programme in return for conventional military hardware and security assurances. The move towards a comprehensive test ban treaty (CTBT) was actually an attempt to formalise these attempts.

When the CTBT was drafted in 1996, India objected to it on various grounds, the primary one being that it allows the present nuclear powers, to maintain and even upgrade their arsenals.

Has the bomb made India more secure or vulnerable? With Pakistan also having exploded its own devices, would it foment an arms race? A nuclear India and a nuclear Pakistan are more likely to desist from attacking each other than a non-nuclear India and a non-nuclear Pakistan.

Like in the US, India can utilise its nuclear energy to generate power that is needed in several industries. It has better simulation capabilities than Britain and China, and can be ranked third in nuclear technology.

❖ ❖ ❖ ❖ ❖

28. India's Space Programme

The Indian Space Research Organisation (ISRO) has come a long way from a modest beginning with the Nickle Appache rocket launch with sodium vapour payload in 1963. The launch vehicle development programme later shifted from Thumba to the Sriharikota launching station in 1969.

The development flight of SLV-3 in 1983 resulted in the satellite sending home more than 2,500 pictures. In 1992 ISRO launched the ASLV-3 which hoisted the Stretched Rohini Satellite. Its successor launched in 1994 was a success.

The Vikram Sarabhai Space Centre at Thumba, Thiruvananthapuram, is the national centre providing technology base for the country's indigenous satellite launch vehicle development efforts like PSLV. It also supports the Thumba Equatorial Rocket Launching Station, the international sounding rocket range, the Rohini Sounding Rocket Programme, and space physics Laboratory.

The satellite INSAT, established in 1983 with the commissioning of INSAT-1 B, is a joint venture of the Department of Telecommunications, Indian Meteorological Department, AIR and Doordarshan.

The INSAT system provides uninterrupted services to the country in the vital areas of telecommunications, TV broadcasting, meteorology, disaster warning and distress alert. With four remote sensing satellites in orbit, India has the largest constellation of such satellites in operation.

The PSLV is technologically the most challenging endeavour of the Indian space programme till date. GRAMSAT is tailored to meet the basic requirements of rural areas for disseminating culture and region-specific knowledge on health, hygiene, environment, family planning, better agricultural practices, etc. It incorporates features for providing continuing education for special social groups, industrial workers and others.

❖ ❖ ❖ ❖ ❖

29. Scarcity of Drinking Water

About 97 per cent of the earth's water is salt water; of the remaining three per cent, only a fraction is accessible for use. Water is unevenly distributed, both within countries and within regions of the world.

Over one billion people lack access to an adequate supply of safe water. Some countries, comprising 40 per cent of the world's population, are already suffering from serious water shortages. A report considered by UN says that unless some stringent measures were taken, by the year 2025, two-thirds of the world's population will live in countries facing moderate to severe water stress.

Water stress and water scarcity can change from year to year or from season to season, depending on population growth levels and on the demand from various sectors that use water. Sweden is water rich; Jordan and Israel are water-poor. They are at opposite ends of a sharply divided spectrum of water 'haves' and 'have nots'.

By the end of this century, a large number of countries will enter the category of water-scare nations. Global water consumption is rising by 2 to 3 per cent every year. Although statistics for water use differ significantly in terms of continent, region, country, area and type of use, according to the World Health Organisation, the total world demand for water increased by six times between 1900 and 1990 – more than double the rate of population growth for the same period!

In India, water is becoming a rare commodity now a days. The level of underground water is going down. As the population is increasing, the demand for water too is rising. When there is less rainfall, rivers, wells and lakes dry up. Even then people waste water.

The concept of rain-water harvesting has add a new dimension to conservation of water. Non-government organisations can do a lot in popularising this in rural areas, as is being done in many metropolitan cities.

❖ ❖ ❖ ❖ ❖

30. AIDS

AIDS – acquired immuno-deficiency syndrome – is the late stage of infection with HIV (human immunodeficiency virus). AIDS can take around seven to ten years to develop after infection with HIV.

HIV is transmitted through semen and vaginal fliuds, infected blood and blood products, infected mother to her baby – before birth, during birth or through breast milk.

HIV is not spread by drinking water or eating food from the same utensils, sharing toilets, shaking hands, hugging or kissing, donating blood, working with people who are HIV infected, massage and rubbing each other's bodies, swimming in pools used by people with HIV/AIDS, through mosquito bite, socialising or casually living with people with HIV/AIDS. It is not spread by sitting next to someone who is infected, coughing or sneezing, public transportation, public telephones, restaurantes, air, etc. But if you have any cuts or sores on your hands, make sure they are covered with band-aids.

The first case of AIDS in India was reported in 1986 from Chennai. Since then there has been an increase in the number of HIV infections over the years.

A host of opportunistic infections are seen in increasing number in the AIDS patients. Tuberculosis is the major infection accounting for about 60 per cent of the total cases.

According to the medical research community worldwide, the AIDS epidemic is a grave problem, with the potential to become the worst plague this species has ever known. Greater sums of money should be utilised for treatments and vaccines. On the other hand, while it does not seem likely we will find either a cure or a vaccine in the foresseable future, it may be that truly effective treatments that can indefinitely prolong the life of AIDS victims may be discovered in the next few years.

❖ ❖ ❖ ❖ ❖

31. Importance of Science

Science is a systematic classification of experience. It is organiseed knowledge that is accurate in observation. Every great advance in science has issued from a new audacity of imagination.

Science has made very useful contributions to our world. It has armed man with inventions, which are no less than miracles. We should be ever grateful to Thomas Alva Edison who gave us so many inventions. Others like Michael Farraday, Graham Bell, Marconi, Louis Pasteur, Jenner, Huxley, etc. have contributed towards better living standards with their useful inventions.

Electricity is one such invention that has benefited mankind to a great extent. Electric cranes, trains, electric gadgets, printing presses are some of the inventions that have made life cushy.

Science is indeed a blessing for mankind. Motor cars, trains, aeroplanes, ships are swift means of travel and transport. The foray into space is another landmark in the age of science. The launch of satellites into space has improved the telecommunication system.

The inventions of the telegraph, wireless and telephone have made it possible to transmit messages to any corner of the world within seconds. Radio, television and computer have added variety to the forms of educational aids and recreational benefits.

The wonders of science in the field of medicine and surgery are to be seen to be believed. Science has helped man to control many diseases like smallpox, typhoid, cholera, malaria and so on.

The various sources of energy that are renewable have been harnessed by man for various purposes, thanks to science. Atomic and nuclear energies have also been put to useful purposes, through they can be destructive if used for war purposes. With research in science and technology being an ongoing process, man can hope for better and better means of development for a safer and peaceful life for man on earth.

32. The Age of the Computers

The twenty-first century is witnessing a computer revolution in which information processing and retrieval are being reliably done at incredible speeds.

Today, microprocessors can be found in children's toys, world processors, pocket calculators, industrial robots, home appliances, etc. (to mention a few of their innumerable uses), and there is practically no machine, instrument, control equipment or information system that does not have a microprocessor in it.

The first four generations of computers were based on the technology of the age to which they belonged. They were thus based on the vacuum tube technology, the transistor and printed circuit technology, the integrated circuit technology and the Very Large Scale Integrated (VLSI) technology, respectively, during the last four decades. Presently the development has entered areas of 'Artificial Intelligence'. These are generally called fifth generation computers.

Computers are analog or digital machines. Those converting numbers into physical quantities, which can vary continuously within a range, are called analog computers, while those using members, which are discrete values, are called digital computers.

While analog computers are for specific scientific/technological operations, such as solutions of differential equation, etc. in the fields of hydrodynamics, aerodynamics, industrial control, etc., digital computers are universal in that they have applications not only in the scientific field, but also in the fields of business and administration. Further, due to their superior flexibility and accuracy, digital computers dominate the contemporary scene. The latest of these are called microcomputers.

The origins of the present technological revolution can be traced to the 1930's. The Harvard Mark I Computer designed by Howard Aiken is the world's first digital computer which made use of electromechanical devices. It was developed jointly by the International Business Machines (IBM) and the Harvard University in 1944.

Computerware can be divided into hardware and software. The five functional units of a computer built with electronic circuits and electromechanical devices constitute the hardware; software refers to range of programmes used on the hardware to perform various functions.

E-mail and websites have made communication easy and widely accessible. Computer networks are used for coordinating things at distant places.

Computers are being used on a wide scale in assembly plants, such as shipbuilding, manufacturing, railways, thermal plants, oil refineries, etc.

❖ ❖ ❖ ❖ ❖

33. Sources of Energy

Man is capable of harnessing energy from various sources, like windmill, wood, coal and peat, atom and sun. Amongst these wind is the oldest source of energy in the world.

Ships and yachts were moved by wind with the help of sails, before engines were introduced to run them. Man used the wind for movement from one place to another. It was also the first source of energy, apart from horses and bullocks, to draw water from the well, to grind wheat, etc. Wind mills were common in many countries, especially in Holland. They are still functioning, and are a great attraction for tourists.

Wood replaced wind as a source of energy, as it was available in aundance throughout the world, and also because it could be used anywhere unlike wind that was available only where it was swift and constant. Wood was burnt, and the heat was used to turn water into steam that became a very useful form of energy. This source of energy was used for a very long time in engines, steamers, machines, etc. till coal was discovered as a source of energy.

Coal substituted wood for providing energy. It had an advantage over wood as it was highter and occupied less space for storage, and also gave more heat. Known as Black Gold, it was used in ships, mills, locomotives, etc. It is still used to generate heat for steam that is required by propellers to generate electricity in thermal power stations.

Since coal may not be available all the time, as they are being depleted, man's quest for other sources of energy led him to the discovery of oil below the earth and in the sea bed. In India oil is available in Assam and Bombay high, but most of its requirements are met by oil-rich Arab countries. Since petrol is the highest source of energy, flights and air transport have become feasible.

Atomic energy was then channelised to generate electricity, and many atomic power stations were set up all over the world. Submarines, railways and aeroplanes commenced operations using nuclear power. But the threat of pollution lurks large, and people are again going back to renewable sources of energy like biogas, solar, wind, and so on.

❖ ❖ ❖ ❖ ❖

34. Cloning

Cloning is considered beneficial for mankind as it has more uses than abuses. It is necessary for progress in the quality of life.

The theory of being able to produce a genetic copy (a clone) of another animal has been popular for quite some time. Cloning is nuclear engineering in which the nucleus of a somatic cell is transferred to a denucleated ovum, and the imitation zygote so formed is induced to divide in the test tube. It is implanted into the uterus where it undergoes normal development. The offspring would be an exact copy of the donor of the somatic nucleus.

Ian Wilmut's declared objective for developing this scheme was to clone transgenic animals for large scale production of pharmaceuticals. Even before the announcement of the birth of the cloned Dolly, a sheep, he had created a transgenic cow whose milk contained all the amino acids that a newborn baby needs, and might be used as a substitute for breast milk. After Dolly, he created another clone, Polly, carrying a human gene. More recently, the piglets – Nillie, Christa, Alexis, Carrel and Dotcom – have been added to the new world created by man.

On the positive side of cloning, scientists claim that they create spare-part tissues for repairing damaged brain and other organs that have led to Parkinsons and Alzheimer's diseases. They also believe that they can harvest 'stem cells', the basic cells, from which they can grow any kind of tissue, bone, blood and muscles, and also other body parts or organs for transplant. This would prove beneficial in the cure of kidney, liver or heart disease.

On the negative side, there is a growing concern that these experiments might introduce harmful and uncontrollable microbes. The genetic engineering, by creating the desired trait in the organism of his choice, is playing God. Thoughtful scientists are worried that large scale introduction of altered organisms would upset the balance of nature. They feel that cloning is working against the laws of nature and organic revolution.

❖ ❖ ❖ ❖ ❖

35. Gene Therapy

With the chemical synthesis of the genes in the seventies, hopes were raised about the possibilities of gene therapy. This envisaged replacement of defective genes with normal ones, thus bestowing permanent cure to patients suffering from genetic disorders.

Gene therapy came to age with the involvement of Dr. French Anderson. In 1990, he and his colleagues began to treat patients afflicted with Severe Combined Immuno-deficiency (SCID) disease caused by the failure of the production of the enzyme adenosine deaminase (ADA). This deficiency results in the reduction of disease resistance and makes the body defenceless against infection.

Normal genes for ADA were synthesized and inserted into disarmed viruses. These genetically engineered viruses were then mixed with defective bone marrow cells separated from the patient. Viruses carrying the ADA gene entered the bone marrow cells which thus gained the ability to make the enzyme. A billion such cells were injected into the patient which made recovery possible for the patient. And the first scientifically designed gene transfer experiment in humans was a success.

Transfusion of engineered cells have to be done periodically, and in that sense, gene therapy has not yet provided permanent cure. Although the possibility of the desired gene became clear there was no information about an efficient gene carrier or other modes of transportation of the gene to the affected human ograns or cells. Some of the more adventurous researchers were not prepared to wait until the solution of all problems, and proceeded covertly to treat patients with genetic diseases.

However, gene therapy is becoming popular, and in the USA alone more than a thousand patients are undergoing treatment for various genetic disorders.

❖ ❖ ❖ ❖ ❖

36. Democracy in India

Democracy means the government of the people, by the people, for the people, as promulgated by Abraham Lincoln. It is based upon the conviction that there are extraordinary possibilities in ordinary people.

In our multi-party political system a citizen elects one of the candidates standing for election, regardless of the personal merits of that candidate, regardless of the personal merits of that candidate. No political party would guarantee about his credentials, and whether he has any shady past. The electorate is aware of it all, but finds itself totally helpless when it comes to casting the vote. But then, in our election system, we vote for the party and not pointedly for the candidates representing it. We also know that citizens of high morals and excellence do not become members of political parties.

It is every political party's ambition to get a majority so that it can form the government. We hear of collective responsibility of the cabinet at the centre, where all decisions are arrived at on consensus or unanimity basis. Strange as it may sound, it is a known fact that a minister holds office at the pleasure of the prime minister or the chief minister. The fear of being dropped from the cabinet lurks in his mind constantly, especially if he happens to be a sort of rebel holding radical and independent views. Due to this fear, a minister has no option but to toe the line of the prime minister or chief minister.

While the common man is advised by leaders to maintain discipline, believe in secularism, discard casteism, avoid nepotism, and so on, the politicians themselves are an indisciplined lot. Consider the issues of the Mandal Commission, inter-state river water disputes, practice of religious conversions, communal clashes, and you will realise that the comon man is hit most by these disputes. The heads of the executive and the judiciary look helplessly at the non-execution of the law of the land.

As Calvin Coolidge writes, "It would be folly to argue that the people cannot make political mistakes. They can and do make grave mistakes. They know it, they pay the penalty but compared with the mistakes which have been made by every kind of autocracy they are unimportant."

❖ ❖ ❖ ❖ ❖

37. Cooperative Farming

Daniel Webster aptly describes farmers as : "Let us never forget that the cultivation of the earth is the most important labour of man. When tillage begins, other arts follow. The farmers, therefore, are the founders of civilisation."

India is a land of several villages where farming is the mainstay of the village folk. As an agricultural country, India is gradually progressing towards self-sufficiency, though the conditions for agriculture are not always conducive or favourable for profits.

After independence there have been many positive changes in the agricultural sector. Much has been done for better harvesting methods, though much more needs to be done. The five year plans, started during Nehru's regime, continue till date, focus mainly on agriculture, and there has to be more production to implement the plans. The inadequate funds, distancing of farm technologies from markets, insufficient and untimely supply of credit, and post-harvest losses are the worrying factors.

Cooperative farming is an important step towards a better economy in our country. The farmers get together and form a cooperative society. With their united efforts, the farmers undertake agricultural production. The income and produce are divided among the shareholders according to the shares they hold in the cooperative. The plot of land on which farming is done on a joint basis is held by the farmers.

Cooperative farming is most suitable in a democratic set-up. Even in countries like Japan, Denmark and Russia cooperative farming has been popular.

While such kind of farming is beneficial to the farmers, most of them still like to have individual plots of land and work individually, as they are their own masters, and grow what they want without getting involved in disputes. Being conservative they would not like to share their produce or earnings with others.

❖ ❖ ❖ ❖ ❖

38. Cottage Industries

India is a large populous country where small-scale industries provide employment for multitudes. The small entrepreneur and the cottage industry need to be encouraged to produce more so that the poverty problem eases out.

One of the greatest problems that the cottage industries face is that of finances and non-availability of raw materials. The major financial institutions like banks and life insurance companies can help the villagers. Compact bodies backed by their institutions should be formed at the village level. Village artisans should also be included in these bodies. A planned effort should be made according to the needs and availability of skills in the area. Official delays should be minimised and entrepreneurship should be inspired. A great progress has been made in this direction by the Gujarat Financial Corporation. But the efforts are limited to big urban areas only. Such corporations should honestly enter the rural areas.

The problem of marketing is another great hindrance in the development of this sector. It is closely associated with the lack of talent and technical knowhow resulting in the manufacture of substandard goods. Government and voluntary organisations of technicians and engineers can do a lot in this direction. Training camps can be organised according to the needs of the region. An eye should be kept on the quality of goods.

Small units can be opened as assisting industries and assemblage centres. The brass industry of Moradabad, the lock industry of Aligarh, the match and fireworks industry of Sivakasi, the diamond-shaping industry of Gujarat, the precious stone manufacturing industry of Jaipur are working along these lines.

In the absence of a voluntary or government organisation to manage all the aspects of these industries vested interests have been generated. The poor artisan remains in the background.

❖ ❖ ❖ ❖ ❖

39. Unemployment

While conventional wisdom has it that a person is in a far stronger position if he is in a job, it may not always guarantee that he looks at the widest choice of options. The major cause of employment is the insufficient expansion of opportunities of work in relation to the increasing population of the country.

In view of the underdeveloped conditions of the country, this deficiency can be made up only by a vigorous, adequate and many-sided programme of economic development. The problem of unemployment should therefore be tackled on all fronts and, more practically, by the organised growth of cottage and village industries, on an efficient basis as well as by other production and development schemes, which utilised this labour, increasing the purchasing power of the people, and add to general production.

The problem of employment for those who receive education in schools and colleges is also becoming difficult. The number of such persons has increased out of proportion to the possible opening of the kind sought by them in present conditions, and the quality and kind of education which they receive is, in many cases, not well adapted to the present requirements. The educational system should, therefore, be recognised from this point of view, and the admission to the public services should depend on special tests, merit and ability, and not merely on the possession of degrees.

The major test of the success of any plan is the measure by which one deals with the problem of unemployment. In a welfare state, there should be practically no unemployment, and opportunities for work should be available to all those who desire it. This problem in a vast country like India is big, and cannot be solved fully in a short period of time.

Nevertheless, the aim of social and economic progress must be the attainment of full employment, and steps towards this goal should be taken as quickly as possible. The existence of unemployment is not only a social evil and a burden on the nation but it also comes in the way of fuller production as this productive labour power is wasted.

❖ ❖ ❖ ❖ ❖

40. Elections

There is too much money involved in elections. This is the root cause for most politicians to become corrupt. As William Pitt in 1770 stated, "Unlimited power corrupts the possessor." And power it is that is responsible for so many cases of rigging during elections.

In many states, liquor barons are major financiers, which makes elections a dangerous mix of liquor mafia and illicit money. Can an average citizen become a candidate? No. Our democracy is being corroded by the lure of the lucre, and some of these wealthy magnates are mixed up with criminals. Therefore, while parliament should look at state funding, it should also do only after closing the existing loopholes.

Today, the limit on expenses is Rs. 15 lakh for the Lok Sabha, but this may not include money spent by parties and friends. Therefore, we need to raise the limit, even while making funds easy to monitor so that friends and companies are shut out. State funding is meaningless without this.

But the main political parties are quite happy with the way things are. If this continues, criminals will take over Indian democracy. How can law-makers become law breakers? The parliament is a sacred place.

The suggestion is to block all those against whom charges have been framed for a full trial. If such a law were to be passed by parliament, it will be upheld by the courts because the Supreme Court has laid the doctrine of reasonable restrictions. Your right of candidature can be restricted in order to protect the health of the Indian state. The Indian state as an entity also has rights.

The time has come to impose educational restrictions. An elected member has to read papers on law-making, budget, etc. Will this not tilt the balance in favour of the elite? No, there are educated people available in all sections of society. Today, even a fourth class employee has a postgraduate degree.

❖ ❖ ❖ ❖ ❖

41. Mass Education

The education policy of the government in the post-Independence era has been to provide free and compulsory education to all children, at least up to the elementary stage. Recognising the need for a literate population and provision of elementary education as a crucial input for nation building, the government's stand was endorsed in the National Policy on Education and the Programme of Action, 1992, to work towards provision of education of a satisfactory quality to all children up to 14 years of age before the commencement of the twenty-first century.

Under the present system of mass education by classes, too much stress is laid on teaching, and too little on active learning. The child is not encouraged to discover things on his own. He learns, depending on outside help, not on his own power. Thus he loses intellectual independence and creativity, and the capacity to judge for himself. The over-taught child is later on the man who makes modern democracy the force it is.

Moreover, lessons in class are uninteresting, keeping the child mainly unoccupied, and therefore he gets bored. He is forced to learn what does not interest him. The information acquired mechanically through repetition is easily forgotten. Quite naturally, the child being bored and unoccupied is also mischievous. A strict external discipline becomes necessary to check chaos. The child learns to obey, not to control himself. He loses moral as well as intellectual independence.

We need a new system of universal education. It should be of the same kind that has proved itself so successful in training of the handicapped. We need to change our education system, having a national standard for goals, curriculum or regulations. The commission responsible for education in the country should improve the content of education, raise the standards of student achievement, particularly in testing, increase the time spent on education and provide incentives to encourage more individuals to enter the field of education as well as improve teacher preparation.

❖ ❖ ❖ ❖ ❖

42. Deforestation

Increasing destruction and degradation of forests and greenlands, especially in the Himalayas and other hilly areas, contribute to heavy erosion of top soil, erratic rainfall and recurring floods. It is causing acute shortage of firewood and loss of productivity due to eroded and degraded lands. Another area of concern is degradation of forests due to biotic pressure.

The national forest policy clearly recognised the multiple use nature of forests, rights of local populations, including the indisability of protecting forest resources without their active participation, and the role that forests play in the survival strategies of the poor.

The task of regenerating the degraded forests and lands adjoining forest areas, and implementation of eco-development programmes is being undertaken by the National Afforestation and Eco-Development Board.

Cutting trees has been in practice from ancient time. Despite the loss of national wealth and ecological disturbances it has continued for more than a century. Preservation of forests with their beautiful trees is of prime importance. How aptly George P. Morries says in *Woodman, Spare That Tree*:

Woodman, spare that tree!
Touch not a single bough!
In youth it sheltered me,
And I'll protect it now.

Some of the rare species of animals have also been lost. The major schemes in the wildlife sector concentrate on conservation protection and development of wildlife and its habitat. Forests contain much, though by no means all, of India's biodiversity. The flora and fauna need to be protected at all costs, as some of them are rare species and all the more valuable to the country.

❖ ❖ ❖ ❖ ❖

43. Urbanisation

The old cities were never built to accommodate such a great movement from the rural areas and small towns. The sudden enlargement of residential areas has not been much planned. With the expansion of cities many slums that were on the periphery of the city are now in the midst of developed areas.

Affluence and poverty side by side seems a good adjustment. But the health hazards have not been limited to the hut; they are immediately affected in the better localities too. An epidemic that starts in slums snowballs into the city as well. Moreover, the slums are so congested, and the amenities are so little, that the dwellers are generally on a warpath against one another near water taps.

With all its intellectualism and modern living, urbanisation is responsible for artificiality, breaking of family ties, and utter loss of emotional relations. Freedom from the bondage of old customs and superstitious customs is welcome. But the vagaries of addiction to drugs and psychological problems in the material world of big cities cannot be underestimated. Environmental pollution due to automobiles had added one more misery to the vast expansion of cities.

A young man who moves to the city for education would not like to go back to the rural setting to lead a rough and coarse life. Thus the educated concentrate in the cities only.

No temptation from the government in terms of highest salaries or other facilities leads the doctor, belonging to a rural family, back to his village. For a technocrat, there is no option but to be in a city. Just as there is a desire among the city dewellers to go abroad, there is an equally great desire for the rural youth to gravitate towards urban areas.

Thus the big cities have in their lap a number of different type of people, from a poverty-stricken labourer to a rich industrialist—people belonging to different faiths and interests. They come to cities for different reasons and pleas. For some, it is the glamour, for others it is necessity that brings them together. It is a mixed society living on the same plank. One may ideally call it a unity in diversity. It is nothing like that; there is no sense of unity at all. It is a compulsion forced upon them.

❖ ❖ ❖ ❖ ❖

44. Environmental Pollution

The biosphere, or the ecosystem, is an evolutionary system. It represents a stable balance of various physical and biological factors. Air, water, men and animals, plants and planktons, soil and bacteria are all invisibly interlinked in a life-sustaining system that we call the environment.

In rural areas, more population means more pressure on land, over-exploitation of soil, over-grazing and cutting of trees. This leads to environmental hazards.
More water is consumed by the increasing population. Forest denudation and inconsiderate cutting of trees mean lesser rains.

While man has the right to avail himself of the natural resources available to him, he has overexploited the use of them, leading to an imbalance in the environment. Necessity may have driven him to overuse, but too late in the day it has dawned on him that some resources will soon longer be available to him.

Industries that emit a lot of smoke, especially chemical industries, are mainly responsible for environmental pollution, especially air pollution, creating a dense cloud of smog in the atmosphere.Though industries are necessary for the development of a nation, proper measures must be taken to ensure that the emission levels of smoke and effluent water are controlled and treated before letting them out of the premises. Such pollutions otherwise decrease the oxygen content in the atmosphere, leading to health hazards.

The oxygen level also gets depleted due to deforestation. The government has passed laws to protect the forests, but these stringent laws are flouted by many people. Poor people depend on wood for their domestic purposes, and as a source of energy, driving them to felling of trees for their wood.

Poaching has been widely reported from many game sanctuaries, and the upper crust people are mainly responsible for shooting of the innocent animals, with the connivance of the villagers from the surrounding areas. Many species of animals are near extinction, and the government is now keeping a strict check on poachers who are caught and punished.

Vehicular emissions have added to the woes of the urban population. Pollution of rivers, lakes and other water body sources is an alarming signal. The municipal authorities in change of water supply should tackle this problem of water pollution on a war footing.

❖ ❖ ❖ ❖ ❖

45. Earthquakes

An earthquake is a shaking of the ground caused by the sudden breaking and shutting of large sections of the earth's rocky outer shell. Earthquakes are among the most powerful events on earth, and their results can be terrifying. A severe earthquake may release energy 10,000 times as great as that of the first atomic bomb.

Rock movements during an earthquake can make rivers change their course. Earthquakes can trigger landslides that cause great damage and loss of life. Large earthquakes beneath the ocean can create a series of large, destructive waves called tsunamis that flood coasts for many kilometres.

Earthquakes usually never kill people directly. Instead, many deaths and injuries in earthquakes result from falling objects and the collapse of buildings, bridges and other structures. Fire resulting from broken gas or power lines is another major danger during a quake. Spills of hazardous chemicals are also a concern during an earthquake.

The force of an earthquake depends on how much rock breaks and how far it shifts. On average, a powerful earthquake occurs less than once every two years. At least 40 moderate earthquakes cause damage somewhere in the world each year.

People suffered serious losses in terms of life and property in Lattur in Maharashtra and in Gujarat. Recently, the northern belt of India was seriously affected by an earthquake, the main area being Jammu and Kashmir in India, and a situation prevailed in Pakistan-occupied Kashmir where more than a thousand lives are believed to have been lost.

In a certain way, every act of nature's fury like an earthquake reminds us of two things: One, that nature demands its due respect. Laws of conservation have an underlying spirit of cosmic unity. Second, nature's fury makes no distinction about human divisions, whether they are social, religious or geographical.

As Immanuel Kant says, "Everything in nature acts in conformity with law."

❖ ❖ ❖ ❖ ❖

46. Global Warming

Many scientists believe that human beings may be causing something just as dangerous like climatic changes over this century larger than any, since the dawn of civilisation.

The principal change to date is in the balance of gases that form the earth's atmosphere. These naturally occurring greenhouse gases, including carbon dioxide, methane, nitrous oxide and water vapour keep ground tempratures at a global average of 15° Celcius. Without this natural blanket, the earth's surface would be about 30°C colder than it is today, making the planet a freezing, barren, lifeless place similar to Mars. The greenhouse gases keep the surface warm.

The problem is that human activity may be making the greenhouse-gas blanket thicker. For example, burning fossil fuels throws huge amounts of carbon dioxide into the air; the destruction of forests allows carbon stored in the trees to escape into the atmosphere; and other activities such as raising cattle and plant rice emit methane, nitrous oxide and other greenhouse gases.

Until mankind began burning fossil fuels, greenhouse gases that occur naturally remained in relative balance. A Swedish chemist theorised that increasing amounts of carbon dioxide released into the atmosphere by coal-field industries would cause global warming.

The Inter-government Panel of Climate Change, set up by the UN General Assembly, has listed several likely negative outcomes of global warning: rise in sea levels, change in weather patterns bringing more floods or draughts to some areas, the spread of mosquito-borne infections, etc.

Measures worldwide are being taken to phase out chlorofluorocarbons and other man-made chemicals that deplete earth's protective ozone layer. With such steps as these, some scientists now report that the earth's ozone layer may well be on the way toward a recovery and balance of levels in the atmosphere.

❖ ❖ ❖ ❖ ❖

47. A Dust Storm

A dust storm is always a harrowing experience and a great musiance. it occurs when there is a difference of pressure between two places. Winds carry dust from a place of higher pressure to one of lower pressure. These normally come about in summer.

I was once caught in such a dust storm on a hot day in June. It was bright and hot outside, with not a trace of cloud in the sky. It was around 4 pm that I set out of the office towards home.

I had barely walked for a minute when I felt a gentle but hot breeze caressing my check. I heard the screeching of birds as they flew hither and thither, flapping their wings in desperation. They seemed disturbed.

Looking up, I saw the sky darkening and a storm approaching very fast. Looking around, I stood at the entrance of a shop that was closed. The sun had disappeared behind the duststorm. The wind struck me with all its velocity, howling and shrieking, covering me from top to toe with fine grits of sand. I closed my eyes tightly, sheltering them with my palms, and turned my face towards the shop door so that my back was exposed to the storm.

As the fiery storm blew I heard through the shrieking winds the leaves rustling fiercely, keeping in tune with the howling winds. The storm rose to a gale and eneveloped everything around it.

The storm was terrible and frightening. Nature's fury unleashed volumes of dust on the earth from the sky above. I heard the crackling sound of branches breaking from trees amidst all this din.

Soon the storm died down, as quickly as it had begun. It was followed by a fine drizzle that was scattering in all directions due to the slight wind that accompanied it.

I looked around as I slowly faced the street again. I was struck by the devastation left behind in the trail of the storm—small trees had fallen; branches were broken with a few of them still hanging limply from the trees; sandy deposits were getting cleared by the drizzle and moving slowly with the rain water; a couple of shops with their tin roofs blown away presented a pathetic sight. Some poles that were holding clothelines lay flattened on the ground. Leaves, papers and other light articles lay scattered all around.

I quietly gathered myself and made my way homewards.

❖ ❖ ❖ ❖ ❖

48. Ozone Depletion

Ozone is a form of oxygen gas made up of molecules with three oxygen atoms rather than the normal two. The stratosphere, the layer of the atmosphere between ten and thirty miles above sea level, is rich in ozone. It forms a protective layer around the earth that serves a vital function: it absorbs the wavelength of solar radiation known as ultraviolet-B which damages the deoxyribonucleic acid (DNA), the genetic molecular found in every living cell, increasing the risk of such problems as cancer in humans. Due to its protective function, the ozone layer is essential to life on earth.

There are several reasons for the ozone layer being gradually depleted. The main cause is the overuse of chlorofluorocarbons (CFCs) that are used as refrigerants in air-conditioners and in several manufacturing processes. This was also formerly used as propellants in spray cans. The CFS molecules are harmless until they reach the stratosphere where they break up due to the intense ultraviolet radiations, releasing the chlorine atoms that they contain. These in turn react with the ozone, resulting in plain oxygen molecules that do not absorb UV-B. A single chlorine atom can destroy up to 100,000 ozone molecules in the stratosphere.

There are also other pollutants that are responsible for the ozone depletion. These are nitrous oxide from fertilisers and the pesticide methyl bromide, which are thinning the protective ozone layer in the stratosphere.

Although CFC use has been greatly reduced in recent years, their molecule already released into the lower atmosphere will be moving towards to the stratosphere for decades, further causing depletion of the ozone. As a result, skin cancers, more cataracts and reduced yields of some foodcrops are likely.

By 2015, planes are expected to have doubled their current contribution to the global greenhouse effect. Airplanes emit nitrogen oxides, which not only contribute to acid rain, but also damage the ozone layer. Scientists predict that by 2015 half of the annual destruction of the ozone layer will be caused by air traffic.

❖ ❖ ❖ ❖ ❖

49. Nuclear Pollution

Pollution is probably one of the most glaring problems that has beset mankind, and we ourselves are to flame for the mess we are in today. Amongst the sources of pollution, nuclear pollution can be quite dangerous to lives if not properly harnessed and leak-proofed.

Many countries that are short in coal and oil supplies have turned to nuclear energy due to its great use and effectiveness. It produces more energy than coal or oil, and releases no pollutants into the atmosphere, and is less cancer causing than the burning of fossil fuels. Yet, new plants are being banned from being set up in the US since it has been instituted as being a non-safe and environmentally non-friendly form of energy.

The Countries in the West has started dismantling their own power plants after the serious leakage at Chernobyl in Ukraine in 1986 that spread atomic radiation over Europe polluting the atmosphere in Poland, Austria and France. Thousands of tonnes of milk, vegetables and other edibles had to be destroyed. Radioactivated cattle too were killed and their meat destroyed.

One of the problems of the nuclear power plants is that there is radioactive waste that remains pollutant for thousands of years. The nuclear waste, nuclear disaster and nuclear war — all three can be environmental contaminators — are directly related to each other that all can result in immediate death. Nuclear wastes are the byproducts of nuclear reactions in power plants. Who can manage this waste for such a long period covering so many centuries? In the early sixties, 3,000 tonnes of radioactive waste of Indian Rare Earths in Kerala was dumped into the Arabian Sea, thus contaminating its waters.

In the USA and some European countries, the movement against this hazardous pollutant is active, and orders for new atomic reactors are being cancelled.

In India, there is no such plan to stop new plants being set up. Let us hope that some non-government organisation would force the government to put an end to these hazardous pollutant projects and turn to the safer renewable sources of energy.

❖ ❖ ❖ ❖ ❖

50. Drug Addiction

Drug addiction has become a major problem in the world today. The root cause for this lies in the change of the social fabric in the modern times. The addiction to drugs is a manifestation of many reasons like single parenthood, a promiscuous society, lack of responsibility among teachers, leaders and the mafia goons who run drug trafficking rackets.

Drug addiction is a common cause of the social root that is eating away the roots of a civilisation, whether it is a progressive or a regressive one. The main drug addicts are young men in the 10-25 age group, constituting about 50 per cent of the addiction population. This group includes people from all walks of life, right from students to doctors, engineers, lawyers, and so on.

Once the addict gets hooked on to one of the drugs like heroin, marijuana, hashish or 'brown sugar', it is very very difficult for him to free himself of them. Within three days of consuming any of these drugs, especially brown sugar which is the cheapest, the addict falls a prey to it. It is sad to see so many students falling a prey to such abuse. The majority of them have tried the most common gateway drug, marijuana.

The drug addicts can be cured in a rehabilitation camp. The withdrawal symptoms set in, like vomiting, muscle cramps, convulsions and delirium. In most therapeutic camps, recovered drug users are isolated from eath other. The perspective of the treatment is that the problem is with the whole person and not the drug. The addiction is a symptom and not the cure of the disorder. The primary goal is to change patterns of behaviour, thinking and feeling that predispose drug use.

Drug addiction is a social menace that has to be eradicated at the grassroots level. Voluntary organisations have to pitch in their might with government organisations to tackle this festering malaise that is doing nobody any good. Those close to the addicts should also encourage the addicts to get themselves treated in rehabilitation camps.

❖ ❖ ❖ ❖ ❖

51. Poverty and Wealth

The unequal distribution of wealth in society is unjust and unnatural. Everyone should have an equal share in all the products of social labour. Everything belongs to us. The sum-total of wealth should be distributed in the spirit of love and social service, as the income of the family is spent among its members at present.

Andrew Carnegie rightly says in his *Gospel Of Wealth*, "Surplus wealth is a sacred thrust which its possessor is bound to administer in his lifetime for the good of the community."

The father of a family does not starve some of his children or give more to others who are pampered. The wealth of the whole world is the property of all who live on the earth. The very poor, who lack even the necessities of life, are therefore unjustly deprived of their share. They are robbed of what is their due. Some rich people have too much wealth, while the poor are given too little. Therefore, if you belong to the upper middle class or the wealthier group of capitalists and landlords, you are called upon in the name of justice to give back what is due to those whom you have deceived. You possess more than enough; you have the necessary comforts and business of civilised life, while others cannot even have access to even the basic amenities. A part of what you call your money really belongs to them. You have stolen it from them by force or fraud.

It is therefore your duty to restore that money to its rightful owners by giving alms, gifts and donations to the poor in your neighbourhood. The feeling of pity moves you to give something. Then increase your gift to a very good amount when you understand that justice demands the immediate repayment of other people's money. Make haste to give away your superfluous wealth, or live in shame and sin as thieves or frauds.

❖ ❖ ❖ ❖ ❖

52. Loudspeaker Menace

Noise pollution is an environmental issue that needs to be curbed using stringent measures. Loudspeakers also compound the menace of unchecked noise.

Loudspeakers are widely used in cities and smaller towns and have become part and parcel of our life in the present day. They can be heard blaring away at social functions like birthdays, marriage ceremonies or political parties or meetings. The larger the gathering, the louder is the music and the festivities. But the ban of its use after 10 pm is a blessing for most of the citizens.

During public speeches indoors or outdoors, the loudspeaker is a useful gadget, and also a necessity. It helps sound to reach the people sitting quite far away from the podium from where a person is giving his address or speech. During election time, loudspeakers are a common fare during which automobiles and others modes of transport are seen carrying loudspeakers, propagating their parties achievements, and soliciting votes for the candidates. Politicians and party workers are seen addressing rallies or large gatherings, using the loudspeaker to reach across to the remote people, justifying their party stand, the merits of voting for their party, and so on. In this sense, the loudspeaker is a boon.

But there is hardly any need to belt out loud music or propaganda songs before and after a speech. Not everyone loves to hear cine music or party songs. Most people would like to enjoy the peace and silence that gives solace to everyone, especial the old people who like to have their own quiet moments without being forced to listen to unwanted blaring music.

There are other people too who would like to have quiet moments of their own. Students studying for exams, people wanting to pray or meditate, the sick and infirm who would like to sleep, babies and infants whose sleeping hours are not disturbed, etc.

As serious-minded citizens of India, it is our bounden duty to ensure that we do not disturb the peace and tranquillity that everyone has a right to.

❖ ❖ ❖ ❖ ❖

53. Hazards of Smoking

It is very easy to acquire bad habits, such as eating too many sweets or too much food, or drinking too much fluid of any kind, or smoking. The more we do, the more we tend to like doing it; and, if we do not continue to do it, we feel unhappy. Addiction to anything should not become a way of life.

Smoking is a habit difficult to give up. They say, once a smoker, always a smoker. It is a large issue within the college, and even high school, community. Many teenagers start smoking just for fun, and end up becoming addicts to it. Any age is an appropriate age to begin smoking, but teenagers are more gullible and fall a prey to this menace, as cigarettes are extremely addictive. Some of them get hooked on to it after smoking a few times during parties or social get-togethers, just because they did not want to become 'social outcasts'.

Smoking is a habit that is cultivated by people from all sections of society. It is an irony despite all the propaganda that smoking is injurious to health. Newspapers and magazines were carrying advertisements by various companies for promotional strategies till recently when government clamped down on them and banned their advertisements. Even without promotional marketing gimmicks, the tobacco companies make huge profits simply because so many people have cultivated the habit of smoking, and thereby the sales of cigarettes have increased considerably.

Smoking causes damage to the lungs, causes emphesema, and is also one of the causes for cancer. Concrete measures must be taken to prevent to eradicate this evil among the citizens. The implementation of 'no-smoking zones' is not very effective, because there is no crackdown by authorities to nab the culprits or the violators of the rule.

Even those who don't smoke are liable to be affected by the smoking whose harmful puffs released in the air are breathed by those present there, thus leading to 'passive' (non-smokers) ones getting affected. A persons has every right to chastise a smoker who is found smoking in public places, for the government has banned smoking in public places.

❖ ❖ ❖ ❖ ❖

54. Joint Family System

The joint family system is gradually becoming non-existent the world over. Though still the norm in most villages in India, in urban areas, very rarely do you find the joint family system prevalent.

When the youngsters in the family complete their education, they are off in search of lucrative jobs which may entail their setling elsewhere.

The girls may get married and live with their husbands where they are employed. The boys in the family leave their home and settle down where they get a job. Once he marries, he stays with his wife, and later his children are born who stay with them till they too grow up and leave their homes.

In the West, very few families live together in a joint family set-up. This is because the government provides food to all those who are unemployed which they may not get if they live in a joint family.

There are various advantages and disadvantages of a joint family system. Let us first look at the positive aspects. The family remains united, as there is a lot of interaction within the families. The children are encouraged to share everything they have. They learn to encourage each other during illness or when one feels down in the dumps. They learn to celebrate functions and festivals in the spirit of bonhomie, and give and take.

The elders in the family also have each to rely upon each other during times of adversities, or to share in the joy of some happy occasion. Through thick and then they learn to stand by each other, and to shelter their kith and kin from the abuses of society.

The negative side to a joint family system is the bickering that sets in among brothers and their wives due to too much interference amongst themselves. Privacy is denied as each person is constantly being watched by other members of the family. A couple may like to go out on a holiday on their own with their children, but there is a delicacy is not asking other family members to join them. They feel obliged to invite them too. If one has a very lucrative job, while another is not able to earn much, a sense of superiority and inferiority complex respectively sets in. One may indulge in buying luxurious items, while another may be constrained to simply restrict himself and his family as he cannot afford anything beyond that.

Circumstances more than preferences are largely responsible for the joint family system gradually fading away.

❖ ❖ ❖ ❖ ❖

55. Unrest among Students

Student unrest has become a common feature of education all over the world. The good old days of strict obedience and deference shown to teachers and lecturers are things of the past. This is a sorry state of affairs when the present generation of youth are relied upon to be the future leaders of a nation.

A student is not an exclusive entity in himself. He lives in a society where he interacts constantly with his own kith and kin, his friends and others, like teachers, peons, neighbours, vendors, and so on. He is influenced by them to a certain degree, and imbibes both virtuous and negative aspects from them.

In today's society, we see many students spending or wasting their time on strikes and agitation when they should be in class pursuing better interests. They are a misguided lot, and a lackadaisical attitude on the part of teachers and principals is partly responsible for such a state of affairs. Consider the announcement of the implementation of the Mandal Commission during the V.P. Singh government, which favoured over 60 per cent reservation for the backward classes. The reaction among students was a spate of self-immolations.

Students are also politically motivated, and are seen joining demonstrations, slogan shouting, taking out processions against the government, damaging and looting public property. This is compounded by their resorting to addiction of drugs, alcohol and smoking. Such types of behaviour indicate a disturbed and restless mind.

Our educational system needs to be revamped. Students are compulsorily made to learn subjects that have no bearing on the course that they want to pursue, or to their practical life. This leads them to frustration.

The home atmosphere is also a cause for unrest among students. When they are neglected by their parents who have hardly any time for them due to their own social engagements, they are left free to engage in their activities some which may not be desirable. So you find them going astray, unchecked by any restraints and supervision.

It is, therefore, essential this type of negligence is set right, and that the tremendous potential of the youth are put to better prospects, both at home and at the educational institution.

❖ ❖ ❖ ❖ ❖

56. Vocational Education

According to Emerson, "The things taught in schools and colleges are not an education, but the means of education." Education is always an ongoing process, where a person learns something each day of his life.

Education is necessary for all-round development of a being. Success, name, fame, prosperity all accrue if one has proper education. For the success of any democracy education is essential.

Every person has a desire to become something big in life and hope to benefit mankind and his nation in some special way. He may like to be a teacher, or an engineer, a doctor, a politician, a bureaucrat, a defence personnel, a scientist and so on. Professional courses take four to five years for completion, and specialisation in a particular field may taken another three to seven years.

There are many students who do not have the resources to pursue professional courses that cost the earth, so they prefer taking up some vocational course that is within their means. Educational institutions offering vocational courses for graduation and postgraduation levels have a wide list of options, like mechanics, textile designing, and electronics, secretarial practices, journalism, ceramics, architecture, and so on. These courses gear them towards becoming independent, gainfully employed in a particular vocation or profession.

As Bacon says, "Reading maketh a full man; writing an exact man; and conference a ready man. Universal suffrage, without a vocational education, would be a curse. Many industries and companies take up training and educating, side by side, of children who have completed their high school level or graduation, and then absorb them in their own organisations. This ensures that they have skilled personnel in that particular field for which training and education were given.

Let us hope that vocational education becomes popular in India.

57. Women's Education

There is a lot of emphasis today in India on enrolment and retention of girl child in formal and non-formal schooling, recruitment of rural woman as teachers, and removal of gender bias in the curriculum.

It is the height of selfishness for men, who fully appreciate in their own case the great advantages of a good education, to deny these advantages to women. There is no valid argument by which the exclusion of the female sex from the privilege of education be defended.

It is argued that women have their domestic duties to perform and that, if they were educated they would bury themselves in their books and have little time for attending to the management of their households. Of course it is possible for women, as it for men, to neglect necessary work in order to spare more time for reading sensational novels. But women are no more liable to this temptation than men, and most women would be able to do their household work all the better for being able to refresh their minds in the intervals of leisure with a little reading.

Education would even help women in the performance of the narrowest sphere of womanly duty. For education involves knowledge by which health may be preserved and improved, and enables a mother to consult such modern books as will tell her how to rear up her children into healthy men and women, and skilfully nurse them and her husband when disease attacks her household. Without education, she will be vulnerable to exploitation by quacks who pretend to work wonders by charms and magic.

Also one of a woman's highest duties is the education of her children at the time when their mind is most receptive to education and instruction. A child's whole future life, to a large extend, depends on the teaching it receives in early childhood, and it is needless to say that the first foundation of education cannot be well laid by an ignorant mother. On all these grounds, educating women is a vital necessity.

❖ ❖ ❖ ❖ ❖

58. Adult Education

Since the inception of the National Literacy Mission in 1988, more than 60 million persons have been made literate under the Adult Education Scheme. There are still many who downgrade the value of education and that it is not necessary for everyone, like, for a shopkeeper, a farmer, a sweeper, a maidservant, a mason and so on. Knowledge is too for advanced today for a man to gain without its specialised branch. Literacy is vital for every citizen.

Farmers in India, in ancient times, were illiterate and were cheated out of their land, and exploited, suffering injustice. Unscrupulous landlords deprived them of their rights, moneylenders and middlemen got their thumb impressions on false documents of possession.

With the spread of adult education, bonded labour, economic slavery, superstitious beliefs are on the wane. The problem with adult education though is that these adults have to earn their bread too. They can be taught only during their spare time near their houses. Non-government organisations can achieve this.

Being illiterate they need to be educated about family planning too, as they usually have large families in the false belief that the more children they have the more income they will have with all their children earning.

As the adults form 40 per cent of the population, most of them living in villages, they are uneducated, hence, all the more need for adult education. In cities the uneducated constitute the slum dwellers, pavement hawkers and coolies at railway platforms. These are mostly engaged in manual work. So what kind of education do they need? Not anything technical like history, science or economics. The simple 3R's would be enough to get them going. They should be given knowledge about their country, the idea of democracy, health and hygiene, and the value of education for children and women too.

States are now giving a lot of importance to adult education also. The Literacy Mission Scheme is gaining grounds, and we hope that Indian adults are all educated soon.

59. The Importance of Newspapers

Newspapers are the world's mirrors. They are the lifeline of society, and our greatest friends. They play a vital role in creating pupil's awareness of policies and programmes for their development and in motivating them to be active apartners in the nation building endeavour.

Newspapers are instrumental in bringing the whole world within the reach of the common man every morning. The various events that are taking place around the world are brought to your doorstep, or to you through the computer.

Every newspaper has various sections catering to the interests of everyone – political news, international events, society interests, sports economic and business section, news, fashion, cartoons, and so on. Advertisements are helpful for those in search of jobs, houses or sites, grooms or brides, educational options, etc.

Besides these, newspapers also serve the purpose of awakening the conscience of man. Riots, disasters such as floods, earthquakes, wars, deaths etc. are covered well by news reporters, and one gets first-hand information of these as they happen.

Most children and adults now-a-days are forgetting the newspaper's role and its importance. Television has taken over from newspaper, and some children and people prefer and watch rather than read. But TV news cannot be as descriptive as the news covered by newspapers. Another advantage of newspaper over TV is that a newspaper can be read at any time of the day, while you have to wait for the news at particular hours of the day. The Sunday supplement paper provides a lot of features that are interesting and educative. Therefore, newspaper reading should be encouraged among all age groups of people to ensure national consciousness in the country.

Newspapers are a better source of propaganda than a radio. Today the press controls public opinion and public opinion controls the government. A newspaper should not be biased, but should report impartially and independently.

Newspapers are published in different languages, and many of them have editions that come out in different states. Such editions focus more on the local news than other regional news.

Newspapers are not limited to presenting political and socials aspects of society. They cover economic problems, educational schemes, health, sports, etc.

President Jefferson once wrote, "Were it left to me to decide whether we should have a government without nespapers, or newspapers without government, I should not hesitate a moment to prefer the latter."

❖ ❖ ❖ ❖ ❖

60. Libraries

Public libraries in some respects serve the same purpose as educational institutions. It is the place where people come to collect material for reference work and for knowledge. It is really one of the most useful institutions in the world.

A library is normally well stocked with all types of books, including the rare ones, and also the expensive ones. Thus everyone has access to these books which otherwise would not be available, or probably be beyond the reach of the common man cost-wise. In this sense, libraries can afford to purchase the rare and expensive books, thus making them available to the general public.

Libraries also have sets and volumes of dictionaries, encyclopedias and other reference books which require a lot of storage space. So a library is an ideal place for such books. Since individuals cannot afford to possess all of them, they can avail of them in libraries.

A library is an ideal place to study and make references as there is silence and no disturbance. Tables and chairs are provided, and one can spread one's notes on the table and carry on one's work without the fear of being disturbed.

Students and scribes are the ones who frequent libraries the most. New materials on different subejcts is now available. Many well established libraries in the West also stock computers, compact discs,

CD-Roms, Xerox machines so that one can have print-outs of the necessary materials that are required for one's reference.

While many libraires are open to the public, some are exclusive, and by paying a nominal sum of money one can get membership to it. By paying a small amount one can derive enormous benefits from it.

In every library there is a librarian who helps you to locate the book you seek. If a new look has been released and it is not there in the library, you can apprise the librarian about it, and he will soon make it available to you for reference.

As good citizens, it will be each one's responsibility to see that the books are handled with care to preserve them for posterity.

❖ ❖ ❖ ❖ ❖

61. Pleasures of Reading

Happy is the man who acquires the habit of reading when he is young. He has secured a lifelong source of pleasure, instruction and inspiration. So long as he has his beloved books, he need never feel lonely. He always has a pleasant occupation of leisure moments, so that he need never feel bored. He is the possessor of wealth more precious than gold.

"Reading is to the mind, what exercise is to the body," so says Addison in *The Tatler*. Ruskin calls books "Kings" Treasuries — filled, not with gold and silver and precious stones, but with riches much valuable than these – knowledge, noble thoughts and high ideals. Poor indeed is the man who does not read, and empty is his life.

The blessings which the reading habit confers on its possessor are many. Provided we choose the right kind of books, reading gives the highest kind of pleasure. Some books we read simply for pleasure and amusement, for example, good novels. And novels and books of imagination must have their place in everybody's reading. When we are tired, or the brain is weary with serious study it is a healthy recreation to lose ourselves in some absorbing story written by a master hand.

But to read only books of fiction is like eating nothing but cakes and sweets. As we need plain, wholesome, food for the body, so we must have serious reading for the mind and here we can choose according to our taste. There are many noble books on history, biography, philosophy, religion, travel and science which we ought to read, and which will give us not only pleasure but an education. And we can develop a taste for serious reading, so that in the end it will give us more solid pleasure than even novels and books of fiction.

Nor should poetry be neglected, for the best poetry gives us noble thoughts and beautiful imaginings clothed in lovely and musical language.

Books are the most faithful of friends. Our friends may change or die, but our books are always patiently waiting to take us. They are never cross, peevish, or unwilling to converse, as our friends sometimes are. No wonder a reader becomes a book-lover.

❖ ❖ ❖ ❖ ❖

62. Poverty

People moan about poverty as a great evil; and it seems to be an accepted belief that if people only had plenty of money, they would he happy and useful, and get more out of life.

As a rule, there is more genuine satisfaction in life, and more obtained from life in the humble cottage of the poor man than in the palaces of the rich. I always pity the sons and daughters of rich men, who are attended by servants, and have governesses at a later age; at the same time I am glad to think that they do not know what they have missed.

It is because I know how sweet and happy and pure the home of honest poverty is, how free from perplexing care and from social envies and jealousies – how loving and united its members are in the common interest of supporting the family—that I sympathise with the rich man's boy and congratulate the poor man's son. It is for these reasons that from the ranks of the poor so many strong, eminent, self-reliant men have always sprung. If you will read the list of the "Immortals who were not born to die", you will find most of them have been born poor.

It seems nowadays a matter of universal desire that poverty should be abolished. We should be quite willing to abolish luxury; but to abolish honest, industrious, self-denying poverty would be to destroy the soil upon which mankind produces the virtues that will enable our race to reach a still higher civilisation than it now possesses.

It is quite true that there are in this country a small number of rich people; but they are so few in comparison with the whole population that even if they were to share out all their wealth among the rest, it would make very little difference.

As Emerson says, "The greatest man in history was the poorest."

And Locke says, "All wealth is the produce of labour."

So get name and wealth, if possible, with grace.

❖ ❖ ❖ ❖ ❖

63. Alcoholism

It is not difficult to pick up bad habits such as smoking, over-eating, eating chocolates chewing gum or even drinking too many cups of tea or coffee. The more we resort to these, the more we want to go on with them all. And if we don't continue with the same quota of each, we feel unhappy, and some people could even turn violent and depressed.

One of the most widely known habits is drinking liquor, especially the cheap ones, such as arrack, by the labour class and villagers all over India. Even some women consume liquor.

Drinking alcohol comes with many responsibilities. Many teenagers believe that there is a thing such as being responsible while drinking. While drinking, teenagers are often put into situations where they act irresponsibly.

Drinking is a social evil that is a menace to society. The social effect of drinking is very dangerous. The slum dwellers are the main addicts to this poisonous quaff. The hunger for sex among drunkards has resulted in the development of flesh trade.

Drinking results in a number of diseases that are incurable, leading to failure of functioning of the liver, kidney, stomach and lungs. The intoxicants start to gradually drink more concentrated doses as they become addicted alcohol.

The indigenous liquor sold under government contract gives more satisfaction to the poor heavy drunkards who otherwise cannot afford to purchase the sophisticated rum or whisky. They even resort to spurious liquor like hooch. Many deaths have been reported to such indulgence in consuming the spurious types of liquor. The government has to impose prohibition in all states, and crack down mercilessly on the violators, be they ministers or ordinary folk.

❖ ❖ ❖ ❖ ❖

64. Pets

Many upper middle class Indian families would have one of the four categories of pets in their home. The first choice is for some kind of dog. The next preference is for cats. The third category of pets is birds. The last choice is fish.

Dog lovers sometimes are amazed that anyone could even touch an animal like a cat. The relationship that householders develop with a pet dog is amazing indeed. As days pass by the children would get so attached to a dog that they cannot live without seeing the dog first thing in the morning, or the first to be greeted when they return from school, And, if by some chance, the dog gets lost, they would be devastated and refuse to eat or do any homework until the father runs out, traces the dear fellow and brings him back.

Many people love to have cats as their pets. You can see them often silently walking in and out of houses, or curled up at the feet of their masters. They are fond of chasing squirrels and rats or mice. You can hear them purring when they are pleased, or you can see them stretching languorously when they wake up from their sleep. They can be quite ferocious when enraged, and ready to pounce on one.

Birds are mostly kept in cages where they are fed daily. They love to eat nuts, small bits of carrots, grains, etc. Parrots are everyone's favourite as they are the most talkative among birds. Some have varieties of birds in different cages which add colour to one's house.

Nowadays, it is quite common to see all an aquarium in many houses. There are a variety of fishes in the aquariums. The gold fish is everyone's choice. There are small and big, lean and fat fishes. They are fed everyday, and the water in the aquarium cleared once in 10 or 15 days.

Pets are additional welcome members in a family, as they bring joy to their masters.

❖ ❖ ❖ ❖ ❖

65. Family Planning

The population of India is increasing at a fast rate, and is own expected to overtake that of China's which has the largest population in the world at present. This is population explosion.

At present the population of our country is inching towards the one billion mark. Control over diseases is one of the causes for this explosion. Medical science has made progress, and powerful drugs to cure diseases have been invented. There are better medical services and facilities, and epidemics are rare.

While the death rate has decreased, the birth rate should also be checked. People should be educated about the need of family planning. The advantages of small families should be focused on, and the uneducated made aware of it.

The most important task before the nation is to check the increase in our population. The people in industrialised countries, like the USA and Europe, are conscious about population growth.

The population growth has resulted in a wide gap between the earnings of the rich and those of the poor, resulting in disparities of economic and social status. People from villages and smaller towns have been migrating to cities in quest of good jobs.

Many methods of birth control are available to the people today. Sterilisation, medicines, condoms can be useful to people in this respect. Late marriages also result in a check in population growth.

But the most essential need for population control is consciousness among the masses. The 95 per cent literacy rate in Kerala is responsible for the lowest population growth rate. It can be achieved in other states too. Family planning should somehow be made mandatory. if China has been able to check its population growth, can India too not do it?

❖ ❖ ❖ ❖ ❖

66. Co-education

It is true that the modern world offers varieties of opportunities for all age groups almost in any field of knowledge. At the touch of a button you can get any information you want, and become knowledgeable very soon. But, it is also possible by touching a wrong button you get access to wrong and harmful knowledge.

While strong-willed young persons could keep away from such evils, the weaklings could become a prey to drugs and pornography, diverting their attention from studies.

Girls would love to mix with boys freely, especially if they study in co-ed schools. Mothers seem to be against this — won't the girls pick up many useful principles from others since they come from different social and academic levels?

It is true indeed. But what if girls go astray, or if limited freedom leads to sexual liberties? Once the reputation of a girl becomes besmirched, her chances of marriage are slim. In our society the grooms want virgins and maidens of purity in mind and habits. It is because of this condition that the parents abhor the idea of much socialising between girls and boys in schools and colleges. Even a teenage elder brother would not allow his sister to ruin her image by free mixing. Admittedly, boys enjoy relatively greater freedom.

But there are a lot of advantages in co-ed schools and colleges. A free exchange of ideas between girls and boys leads to a healthy relationship between them. Co-education should therefore be encouraged right from kindergarten so that the children grow up with the right attitude towards each other. There is healthy competition between them, while at the same time they help each other in various fields of education.

Co-education is becoming increasingly popular. A common school for girls and boys relieves the burden on the government to provide the state with more schools. Girls and boys graduating to a college from such schools have no hassles in relating with other students from other schools in their college. This easy intermingling of boys and girls makes them more confident and outgoing.

❖ ❖ ❖ ❖ ❖

67. Uses and Abuses of Advertisements

You can tell the ideals of a nation by its advertisements. When you want to attract the attention of the public to your products, you advertise in a newspaper, television, radio, journals, pamphlets, hoardings, and so on. Large hoardings and banners carrying the advertisements of products of companies are a common sight along the lanes and streets that crisscross towns and cities.

Television and movies too screen the advertisements. While some may be entertaining and meaningful, others may be cheap and vulgar. Since these are watched by all, both young and old, it is the younger generation of people on whom the impact is more. They are so mesnerised by the product advertised that they pester their parents to buy them the product.

In advertisements in the West, women are exhibited as commodities that sell. They are vulgarly displayed for their sex appeal, and this culture is being aped by other countries in the East too.

The question is, what would be considered as derogatory representation of women? The consensus is that representation, visual or otherwise, intended for public consumption and for commercial gain is derogatory. This means presenting women as sexual objects or commodities, displaying women for sex appeal to attract male audience, showing women in postures of sexual submission or aggression, glorifying their subordination to men leading to their servility.

It advertisements are good and intelligent, they can educate the public, but this is hardly what is projected on television and movie screens. Some of them are so well conceived and presented that they are a welcome change. Some of them can be quite appealing even without visuals by the way they are presented and the construction of slogans that are eye-catching.

When business is good, it pays to advertise; when business is bad you've got to advertise — so goes the saying. By all means advertise, but ensure that you do not violate the indecent Representation of Women (Prohibition) Act of 1986.

❖ ❖ ❖ ❖ ❖

68. The Benefits of Games and Sports

There is no denying the fact that games and sports are essential for one's well-being and all-round development. They symbolise the youth of a nation, as there is physical, mental, emotional and ethical development of the child preserving the youth in him.

Games and sports provide the required physical exercise to make the body of the child strong and muscular. They exercise the lungs, heart and muscles of the child, keeping him fit and healthy.

Games provide recreation and amusement to everyone. Out in the sports field, the participants forget all their worries and find refreshment in the games they play. Games and sports are a pastime that brings relaxation to the mind.

Games also encourage people to cooperate and work as a team. The team spirit in games like cricket, hockey, football, basketball, volleyball, etc. is essential for triumph and success. It is a state of affairs in India that this is not given importance in schools and colleges.

A ration survives when it competes with other nations. The healthy competition between two rival teams is beneficial to both the victorious and the losing teams. Off the field you see so much of friendly interaction and bonhomie amongst the players of both teams.

The games inculcate sportsmanship in all participants. Whether you lose or win the game, you learn to accept the result in good grace, and shake hands with your rivals. The spirit lies in how you played the game, not whether you won or lost it. Teams from other countries come here to play friendly matches.The Olympics and Commonwealth Games are played in the spirit of sportsmanship. They help in developing friendly relationship among the young generation of the world through an environment of goodwill and mutual understanding. This then creates a peaceful atmosphere amongst nations.

❖ ❖ ❖ ❖ ❖

69. Scene at a Railway Station

A railway station is a hub of activity, with people boarding a train or alighting from it. There are people all around, some waiting to see off their loved ones, some waiting to receive their guests or loved ones. There are vendors, coolies, and so on.

The railway station can be a very interesting place. You see all sorts of people on one platform — the young, the old, the rich, the poor, the lame, the healthy, and so on. Some hurry past while some stroll past. Some cry, while others laugh. Some are silent watchers, others are busy jabbering away nineteen to a dozen.

You can see vendors hawking their wares on trolleys. While some sell fruits, some others sell toys, books and magazines, biscuits and sweets, other eatables, drinking water and bottled soft drinks, air-pillows, chains, toiletry articles, etc. There are stalls on the platforms selling hot cups of tea, coffee, milk, or omelettes and sandwiches, or biscuits and cakes. People can be seen at book stalls browsing through books, buying some, while newspapers sell like hot cakes.

There are the waiting rooms which are used by passengers who are transiting, or waiting to board another train which may be hours away. The restaurant run by the Railways is usually a busy spot with passengers stopping by for a bite.

When a train arrives at a platform, there is a lot of expectant faces, both at the platform, and in the train. People on the platform are waiting to receive someone, and look at the train expectantly as each compartment passes by. Those inside too are trying to catch sight of those who have come there to receive them. Coolies can be seen hurrying from compartment to compartment in search of those who want to avail of their services. People can be seen alighting, being joyfully welcomed, hugged or kissed, hands shaken, tears of joy, smiles and laughter, patting each other on backs, some being garlanded.

The departure of a rain is quite emotional for many. They parting of ways, tears in eyes, hands waving in goodbye, last minute hugs and kisses, advices and admonitions from the old to the young, and so on. Indeed, a railways station is a colourful scene, full of life and activity, and never a dull moment.

❖ ❖ ❖ ❖ ❖

70. A Scene at a Polling Booth

Elections in a democratic country are held to elect representatives to parliament or the state assembly. Holding of timely, peaceful elections in a country is the backbone and pillar to the successful functioning of a democratic government. Every citizen, irrespective of caste, age (but not below 18 years), and creed is eligible to vote for the candidate of his choice from his constituency.

A polling scene presents a typical scene of queueing up of people to cast their votes. Tents are pitched and decorated outside the polling booth by political parties. They await the voters who come to the polling booth to exercise their franchise of voting. They have the list of voters for that particular booth. The symbol of their party pinned on to the tents indicate the party the people belong to. When voters come to them to verify if their names are listed there, they generally feel that their candidate will get their votes. Some voters become the cause of quarrel between the workers of the rival parties.

Outside the polling booth, two lines of people can be seen, one consisting of males, and the other of females. Their patience and discipline are worth lauding. There is no shoving and jostling. They enter one by one, looking calm and relaxed. A couple of policemen stand by to see that there are no untoward incidents.

Inside the booth are four to six polling officers, four polling agents and a couple of orderlies. As a person enters the polling booth, he is led to an officer who gives him a ballot paper, after checking his name against the list that he has, and also checking his identity card. He is told to proceed to the voting box and put the stamp on one of the symbols that are in the ballot paper. Then an indelible mark on the left-hand index finger is made. The voter proceeds to the voting box that is placed behind a screen. He stamps his ballot paper on the symbol of the party that he is voting for, folds the paper and drops it into the box.

Very rarely do you find trouble in most booths. Of course, in a state like Bihar, cases of rigging seems to be a common feature. At such times booth capturing, clashes between party workers, police lathi charging the clashers, shouting and beatings – these cannot be ruled out. Then, the results are countermanded, and re-polling is announced at a later date.

❖ ❖ ❖ ❖ ❖

71. A Visit to a Museum

A visit to a museum is a very educative trip. It is the place where artefacts and antiques are on display. By visiting such a place, one's knowledge of one's ancient civilisation increases.

One fine day I decided to visit the museum which I had been wanting to see since I arrived in the city a week ago.

I reached the museum at 2 pm when I knew there would be less crowd. Since entry was free, I stepped into the museum with a lot of interest and curiosity.

The building is, but stands majestically amidst a large area surrounded by lovely lawns and colourful flower beds. It is grand with red sandstone walls with a pretty dome at the top.

Inside the museum is a fine collection of miniature paintings depicting the life of the city during the times of the maharajas. Then there is an array of pottery items, made of clay, terracotta and porcelain. The art and craft section has some beautiful ivory inlaid wood carvings, lovely carved wooden screens, rosewood and teak items and furniture, silk scarves and turbans, swords with ivory handles, sandalwood carvings, and various types of footwear worn by the maharajas.

The next section had works of sculpture, embroidery and stone carvings. These show the rich culture prevailing during that period. A throne made of silver with lovely inlay work was a special attraction.

Passing on to the next room I came across a collection of beautiful crystalware. There were some exquisite chandeliers hanging from the roof-top. Each delicate piece of crystalware was enclosed in a small glass box, with the name of the dignitary who had presented it to one of the maharajas. What amazed me most was the scene of the great *Mahabharata* war presented in the form of crystals. Krishna giving his *hitopadesh* to Arjuna is a stunning piece of art. It had me totally mesmerised. I gazed at in rapt wonder for 10 minutes before I reluctantly moved out of the museum.

As I walked out, I carried with me the picture of the museum with all its valuable artifacts fresh in my mind.

❖ ❖ ❖ ❖ ❖

72. A Visit to a Hospital

A hospital is a clinically clean place, but people visit it only if they are ill, or if they want to visit someone who has been admitted there.

The purpose of my visit there was to visit a close friend who had been injured in an autorickshaw accident. Her condition was bad for she was in a coma since her accident nearly a month ago. This was my second visit to her.

I went to the ward where she was lying. Her sister sat beside her, looking dejected and pensive. I handed her the basket of flowers, and gave her a smile. She got up with a smile and gestured to me to sit in the chair beside the window.

She sat near me and whispered that there was no improvement in her sister's health. She was still on the respirator as one of lungs had been punctured by a broken rib. She had a bandage round her chest. There was no movement of her limbs.

I tried to cheer up the sister, telling her she will recover in due course, as the doctors had predicted. I gave her words of encouragement and told her that all of us in the colony were praying for the recovery of Pramila who was still in a coma.

I sat with her, telling her all the titbits about the colony. She listened passively showing interest now and then. After sitting with her for more than an hour, I decided to go home. I got up and went to the bed to look at Pramila before departing. Her sister, Ananda, too came and stood beside me.

Suddenly, we heard a small moan from Pramila's lips. She moved her head ever so slightly, and then moaned again faintly. Telling me to stay right there, Ananda rushed out and within seconds returned with two nurses. Pramila was again moaning, and one of the nurses rushed out and returned with the duty doctor. He checked her pulse, used the stethoscope and shone his slim torch into one of her eyes. Just then Pramila slowly opened her eyes, stared at no one in particular, and then closed her eyes.

After several moments, she opened her eyes once again, and turning her head slowly, looked around. Seeing Ananda, she smiled weakly and tried to say something. Then closing her eyes she went to sleep.

Ananda was full of joy as much as I was, for now we knew that Pramila was well out of danger. God had listened all our prayers and shown His mercy.

❖ ❖ ❖ ❖ ❖

73. School Annual Day Celebrations

The School Annual Day was held on a Saturday, and we were all eagerly looking forward to the big event. The day finally arrived, and we reached school full of hopes and expectations.

The sports ground where the function was to be held looked clean and colourful. Tents were pitched for the chief guest and visitors. Sofas and chairs were placed neatly, and a table with a small vase of flowers was placed in front of the chief guest's sofa. There were a lot of garden plants in pots decorating the tents. In one of the tents, the school children, who were not participating, sat.

The chief guest was the Inspector General of Police who arrived on the dot at 10 am. He was received by the principal who led him to his seat while everyone stood up, till he was seated. I was given the honour of garlanding him, and he gave me a warm smile.

Soon our cultural programme commenced with our school band marching past the chief guest. This was followed by a drill performed by the primary classes. Then there were various types of dances — the *bhangra* of Punjab, the *kolattam* of Tamil Nadu, another dance by seniors, using poles and depicting the typical dance of the north-eastern states, a nursery action song by the tiny tots which drew a lot of applause from all the visitors and school children. The children looked ever so cute in their long skirts, and half-pants and shirts.

Finally came the much awaited prize distribution ceremony. Starting from the nursery classes, the prizes were given to the deserving students for the various competitions that were held in that academic year. The children proudly accepted their prizes from the chief guest, thanked him and walked back proudly with their treasure.

Finally it was our turn. When my name was called out for standing first in academics. I walked with my head held high and a smile on my lips. I received the cup graciously from the chief guest. Imagine my surprise when my name was once again announced for being the most popular prefect of the year! A day worth remembering.

❖ ❖ ❖ ❖ ❖

74. Children's Day

Every year Children's Day is celebrated on November 14, the day Jawaharlal Nehru was born in 1889. He was very fond of children, and always made it a point to interact with them, especially on his birthday. Hence, November 14 is celebrated as Children's Day.

Nehru was a freedom fighter who, under the guidance of Mahatma Gandhi, steered India to independence from the British monarchy. Even during the days of struggle for independence he did not forget the future citizens of India. He always held them close to his heart, for the little ones gave him great joy.

He would take out a precious few minutes to talk to them whenever he came across them. He was always fond of the little children, and never made any discriminations amongst them. He treated the poor and the rich alike. Seeing their innocent faces and shy smiles he would be moved. They too obviously loved him and endearingly referred to him as Chacha Nehru.

Every year Children's Day is celebrated with a lot of fanfare. Though Nehru is no longer alive, his spirit lives amongst the children of his beloved nation, India. On the occasion, tributes are paid to him, and homages by leading stalwarts are paid at his samadhi by laying of wreaths and flowers. Prayers and hymns are chanted, and bhajans are organised.

Though schools do not function on that day, some schools invite children to the school for celebrations. Dances and songs are organised, games are played, speeches in praise of Nehru are given, and sweets are distributed by the school to the children gathered there.

Many organisations have cultural and variety programmes organised for children. They hold essay, painting and drawing contests for various age groups, and distribute prizes.

Since Chacha Nehru was very fond of red roses, people place a lot of these process flowers at his samadhi, and decorate his large photographs with rose garlands.

❖ ❖ ❖ ❖ ❖

75. Early to Bed and Early to Rise...

Early to bed and early to rise makes a man healthy, wealthy and wise—so goes the proverb.

The great advantage of early rising is the good start it gives us in our day's work. The early riser has done a large amount of hard work before other men have got out of bed.

In the early morning the mind is fresh, and there are few sounds or other distractions, so that work done at that time is generaly well done. In many cases, the early riser also finds to take some exercise in the fresh morning air, and this exercise supplies him with a fund of energy that will last until the evening. By beginning so early he knows that he has plenty of time to do thoroughly all the work he can be expected to do, and is not tempted to hurry over any part of it. All his work being finished in good time, he has a long interval of rest in the evening before the timely hour when he goes to bed. He gets to sleep several hours before midnight, at the time when sleep is most refreshing, and after a sound night's rest rises early next morning in good health and spirits for the labours of a new day.

It is very plain that such a life as this is far more conducive to health than that of the man who shortens his waking hours by rising late, and so can afford in the course of the day little leisure for necessary rest. Anyone who lies in bed late, must, if he wishes to do a full day work, go on working to a corresponding late hour, and deny himself the hour or two of evening exercise that he ought to take for the benefit of his health. But, in spite of all his efforts, he will probably not produce as good results as the early riser, because he misses the best working hours of the day.

It may be objected to this that some find the perfect quiet of midnight by far the best time for working. This is no doubt true in certain cases. Several great thinkers have found by experience that their intellect is clearest, and they can write best, when they turn the midnight oil. But even in such cases the practice of working late at night cannot be commended. Few men, if any, can exert the full power of their intellect at the time when nature prescribes sleep, without ruining their health thereby; and of course the injury done to the health must in the long run have a bad effect on the quality of the work done.

❖ ❖ ❖ ❖ ❖

76. Cleanliness is Next to Godliness

Cleaniness is next to Godliness — Certainly this is a duty, not a sin. It is absolutely necessary for one's self-respect. A person who is clean and tidy in how he dresses up commands better respect from those around him than the one who has a slovenly and unkempt appearance.

It is extremely essential for each of us to keep ourselves, our houses and neighbourhood clean. This is necessary for one's and the nations health and hygiene. Dirt and grime are the causes of ill health and suffering, giving rise to diseases and epidemics. Plagues and epidemics that set in are called by filthy and insanitary unhygienic conditions. So it the duty of every citizen to ensure that public places and our own surroundings are not littered.

A great percentage of our population live below the poverty line. The slums in metropolitan areas are inhabited by these poor people, most of whom have migrated from villages. Unable to earn a decent means of living, they live in shacks and huts, having no proper sanitation or drinking water. The one or two pipes that they have is surrounded by filth and stagnant water infested with mosquitoes and other creatures. Pigs, cows, dogs, etc. add to the filthy conditions.

The uneducated people need to be instructed in civics and clean surroundings. Even the educated are guilty of violating those basic rules. For instance, people go on picnics to public parks, leaving behind litters of papers, foodstuffs and other titbits, attracting crows, dogs and pigs which add to the mess when they scavenge around and spread the litter. Wayside tea stalls and eateries have a lot of garbage in the form of leaf plates, plastic cups and spoons, polythene covers, earthenware, cigarette and beedi stubs, empty coconut shells, biscuit and candy wrappers, banana peels, and so on.

In places like Mumbai, the walls are plastered with graffiti and tobacco and paan stains. Every morning all the streets are swept clean, but within hours we find people littering these streets. In places like Singapore, a person found dropping even a small chocolate rapper is heavily fined. Why is this not imposed in our cities?

Cleanliness of body also leads to cleanliness of the mind, and thereby to the soul. Our states should involve themselves more seriously and bring to book those who are responsible for littering up public places.

77. Mahatma Gandhi

Mohandas Karamchand Gandhi, When first entered public life, he was at first hailed as the Mahatma, and was generally called Mahatma Gandhi. Since his death, he has been universally acclaimed as the father of the nation.

Born on October 2, 1869 at Porbandar, Kathiawar, in India, Gandhi started his public career in South Africa where the white race ruled, and Indians and native Africans alike were treated as slaves and outcastes. He found himself subjected to colour discrimination. He organised the

Natal Indian Congress, and organised the Indian Ambulance Corps for the British in the Boer war.

In 1904, he established the weekly journal *Indian Opinion*. He organised the first satyagraha compaign against the proposed Asiatic ordnance directed against Indian immigrant in Transvaal and then against compulsory registration of Asiatics (The Black Act). For this he was sentenced to two months imprisonment in Johannesburg jail. He again campaigned against General Smuts who broke an agreement, with bonfire of registration certificates, and was again sentenced to jail for three months.

After returning to India, he established the Satyagraha Ashram on Sabarmati River 1917. He led a successful satyagraha for rights of peasants on indigo plantations in Champaran; led a strike of mill workers at Ahmedabad; a satyagraha for peasants in Kheda; organised a nationwide *hartal* by suspension of activity for a day against the Rowlatt Bills; organised satyagraha of non-coopertion; burned foreign cloth in Calcutta; led the historic salt march to Dandi; launched the civil disorbedience movement in 1940 against Britains, and refusal to all Indians to express their opinions regarding World War II; launched the Quit India movement.

Gandhi was arrested and imprisoned several times. He resolved to wear a loin cloth to propagate homespun cotton and to signify his identification with the people. He went on several fasts unto death. He attended several conferences with the British, signed pacts with them, and rebelled against all their proposals.

He brought out *Young India*, an English weekly, and *Navajivan* in Gujarati. He tried to help end untouchability and encouraged spinning and weaving, and handicrafts and cottage industries. He opposed Congress decision to accept division of the country into India and Pakistan. When communal clashes between Hindus and Muslim broke out in many parts of India he undertook fasts till there was peace.

On January 30, 1948, while holding a prayer meeting at Birla House, Delhi, he was shot dead by a Hindu fanatic, Nathuram Godse. The Light of India died with Gandhiji.

❖ ❖ ❖ ❖ ❖

78. Mother Teresa

Mother Teresa was the Florence Nightingale of India, and was known for her selfless services to the upliftment of the poor, the destitute and the sick children. As a world-famous social worker, she has taught us the value of selfless service with a humanitarian approach and a loving touch. She is known for her valuable service in the care of the sick and the diseased, the old and the infirm.

Mother Teresa was born on August 27, 1910, in Yugoslavia. She became a nun at the age of eighteen, and after a year of training, she settled down in Calcutta as a geography teacher at St. Mary's High School.

In 1946, she turned her attention and life towards working in the slums to help the poor. She lived with other nuns in "Nirmal Hriday", and she made it her mission to help the poor and the destitute children. She was soon joined by Sister Agnes, and they tended to nursing the sick and the diseased.

Living in the crowded metropolitan city of Calcutta, Mother Teresa also worked to help the homeless, flood-affected victims, and the orphans. She endeared herself to all the people of all religions and faiths.

Dedicating herself to the upliftment of the needy, Mother Teresa wore the Indian saree and ate Indian food. She learnt Bengali and could speak it fluently. This enabled her to interact easily with the masses.

She had no inhibitions with the diseased people. She was full of sympathy and had a lot of compunction and feelings for the poor and the disease-prone sufferers.

Rightly termed as the 'Angel of Mercy', she founded the Missionaries of Charity. She became a citizen of India in 1962. She set up 570 homes for the poor, spread in about 125 countries.

She won the Nobel Peace Prize in 1979; the Magsaysay Award in 1962; the Pope John XXIII Peace Prize and the Good Samaritan Award in 1979; the Jawaharlal Nehru Award and the Templeton Award in 1972; the Bharat Ratna in 1980; the Order of Merit in 1983; the Rajiv Gandhi Sadbhavana Award in 1993, the Padmashree and many others.

She died in Calcutta on September 5, 1997.

❖ ❖ ❖ ❖ ❖

79. Dr. Bhimrao Ambedkar

Dr. Bhimrao Ambedkar was an Indian jurist, social worker, politician, writer and educationist. But he stands out as the emancipator of the untouchables, and the crusader for social justice.

Born on April 14, 1981, in Maharashtra Baba Saheb Ambedkar graduated from Bombay. He started his career working under the king of Baroda, Siyaji Rao Gaekwad. He worked sincerely and devotedly with a selfless dedication.

He then went to the USA for higher studies, supported financially by the king of Baroda. He researched on Ancient Indian Commerce, and was awarded a doctorate for it. This won him wide accolades from his friends in India and abroad.

From the USA, he went to London and obtained a degree in law. He returned to India and taught law for a few years. He involved himself in politics and fought for social justice and a casteless society. He wanted every citizen of India to enjoy equal opportunities in matters of education, employment and social justice. He shunned the caste system and the discrimination against the low castes and the downtrodden, and air his opinions in public.

He was appointed as chairman of the Constitution Framing Committee, and he framed the Constitution of India which has both rigid and flexible directives. He was offered a post in Jawaharlal Nehru's cabinet which he declined. Instead, he dedicated his life and service to humanity, living as an ordinary citizen among the masses.

Ambedkar died in 1956, but he was awarded the Bharat Ratna posthumously in 1990, after he got recognition as a great leader of India, who had served India selflessly and dedicatedly, working towards the upliftment of the downtrodden and the socially backward.

❖ ❖ ❖ ❖ ❖

80. My First Day at School

My first day at school started when I was four years old. I still remember that day for I was excited about carrying my new school bag.

For the last one year I had been hearing of school, school and school. My neighbour, Raghav, was also four years old, and his parents too were taking him to school.

I wore my new frock, and my mother pinnerd my name on my frock along with my handkerchief. I wore a new pair of white shoes with new white socks. My hair was neatly combed.

I picked up my new bag. It had a small box which contained two biscuits and a sandwich. I had a water bottle too. In another box I had a pencil and an eraser.

I called out to Raghav who came quickly with his parents. We all trooped into the car, my father driving the car. Soon we reached our school, Tiny Tots. I held my mother's hand, and my parents took me to my class. I met my teacher for the first time.

Her name was Janaki, and she bent down and smiled at me. She gave me a chocolate and asked if I would like to see the fishes. She told me first bid goodbye to my parents who would return after two hours to take me home. I did so very reluctantly, but without crying. My mother assured me that she was going to the supermarket to make purchases, and she would return soon with my favourite cheese biscuits.

My teacher took me to the fish pond and showed me the different colour fishes. Then she told me to sit in a chair which was close to her chair. Soon Raghav too came in, and the teacher took him to see the fishes. He sat beside me, and we soon felt at home.

The teacher told us all to stand up and tell our names. Then she taught us a nursery rhyme. We listened to the story she told us, and we felt very happy. She then asked us to come out and play in the ground where there was a sandpit. There were four swings, two seesaws, a jungle jim and two slides. Raghav and I played in the sandpit. I also went down the slide many times.

Then our teacher led us into the class again. She made us all wash our hands at the tap room. Then we sat down and ate whatever we had brought from our houses.

Very soon I saw my parents standing outside, as were other parents. The bell rang, and the teacher told us we could now go home. We picked up our bags and ran out to hug our parents and tell them what all we had done.

It was indeed a great, memorable day in my life.

❖ ❖ ❖ ❖ ❖

81. My Favourite Book

My favourite book till date has been *Tuesdays with Morrie* written by Mitch Albom. This book is an uncredible treasure. When I first read it, I laughed and cried, and have re-read it several times. Every page of this beautiful, moving little book shines with the warmth of unembarrassed love.

The author, Mitch Albom, was given a wonderful gift from his teacher, Morrie Schwartz. He gave his former student a crash course on living: clear and ruthless hindsight on what matters most when your days are numbered.

The author says that the last class of my his old professor's life took place once a week in his house, by a window in the study where he would watch a small hibiscus plant shed its pink leaves. The class met on Tuesdays after breakfast. The subject was 'The Meaning of Life'. It was taught from experiences.

The author goes on to say that no books were required, yet many topics were covered, including love, work, community, family, ageing, forgiveness, and finally death. Although no exam was conducted, one was expected to produce one long paper on what was learned. The last class of the old professor had only one student — the author.

This elegantly simple story is about a writer getting a second chance to discover life through the death of a friend. Morrie's dignity and frankness stirs me every time I read it. All the saints and Buddha have taught us that wisdom and compassion are one. Now along comes Morrie, who makes it perfectly plain. His living and dying show us the way.

It is a book that I would recommend everyone to read. It an eye-opener where I find myself reflecting on what is really important in life.

❖ ❖ ❖ ❖ ❖

82. My Ambition in Life

Everyone has an ambition in life, and I am no different. My greatest ambition in life to is to selflessly dedicate myself to the cause of the gender bias against women in society. As Goethe rightly points out, "The society of women is the foundation of good manners."

Many young women are planning carreers which they hope will make them financially independent. They are averse to be wholly dependent on their husbands. They wish to make their own mark in the world while at the same time making a marriage emotionally fulfilling. For this, they need to have a good education, so that they can learn to stand on their legs independently. They need confidence to handle these dual roles with ease.

Most women no longer see child bearing as their obligatory function. They seem unaware that their plans might be somewhat threatening to the kind of young man they hope to marry. They do not seem to know that some young men are fearful of liberated women, and are happy to marry a girl who will be content to look up to them, and be happy caring for their meals, laundry and children.

My ambition is to see that women and girls are protected from rape, beating and other abuses and violence. I would like to bring about better legal frameworks and policies so that they too have equal rights as men, and have the voice and power to assert their priorities in an increasingly violent world. This can come about if the problem of gender inequality is solved.

It is my greatest ambition to see that women in India, especially those in the backward areas, villages and slums, have access to property and employment, equal wages, to the seats of power, to education, and better living conditions. I would like to take up campaigns to make women aware of their rights so that they are not losers. Woman empowerment would bring about a dramatic reduction in violence against women.

❖ ❖ ❖ ❖ ❖

83. My Favourite Player

My favourite player is the great cricketer, Mohammed Azharuddin. He is the only player in the test cricket to have played against all the test-playing nations, both at home and abroad.

India's most successful captain from Hyderabad, Azharuddin was born on February 8,1963. He started his test debut in 1985 and One-Day debut against England.

He is a right-handed batsman, right arm slow medium pace bowler, and an excellent fielder. His quickness in the field has been an example for youngsters to emulate him.

Azharuddin holds the unique record of three consecutive centuries in his first three tests against England in 1984-85 with scores of 110, 105 and 122 respectively. After Desmond Haynes of West Indies Azhar has taken 8,677 runs in One Day International.

Azhar passed Allan Borders record of 128 catches in the One Day format of the game. He also crossed Border's record of playing most One Day International Cricket. His 55 not out versus Sri Lanka was the fiftieth occasion when he remained unbeaten during an innings. He became the first batsman to do so.

Azhar also became the third batsman to reach his fiftieth 50 in Limited Over Internationals only after Desmond Hayne's fifty-seventh, Aravinda D'silva's fifty-first, and Miandad's fiftieth in the same number of matches.

Azhar had taken 100 catches in Test Cricket. He also tops in One Day with 145 catches. He was the third player after Allan Border and Arjuna Ranatunga to lead the country in 150 One Day Internationals. Till the year 1999, when he played the Dhaka Wills Cup, he was the only player to have played 300 Limited Over Internationals in the world.

Azhar started off 1998 with taking charge of captaincy from Sachin Tendulkar, and won matches in Dhaka, Sharjah, One Day International versus Australia in the Pepsi Cup, versus Kenya in the Coca Cola; versus Zimbabwe, and lost the Sahara Cup.

Unfortunately he was embroiled in a match-fixing scandal during the tour of South Africa to India, and has since been banned from first class cricket.

❖ ❖ ❖ ❖ ❖

82. Knowledge is Power

Power in the past was identified with physical and martial strength. In many cases even today, knowledge is relegated to a second place. It plays an important part in all of man's activities and decisions, for knowledge, too, is itself a power.

Our knowledge is the amassed thought and experience of innumerable minds. To be conscious that you are ignorant is a great step to knowledge.

An Arabic proverb puts it aptly:

He who knows not and knows not he knows not, he is a fool – shun him;

He who knows not and knows he knows not, he is a simple – teach him;

He who knows and knows not he knows, he is asleep – wake him;

He who knows and knows he knows, he is wise – follow him!

Even the monarchs in the past respected those who had knowledge – the rishes and the saints. It was said that a king gets reverence only in his kingdom while a scholar is respected everywhere.

With the growth of scientific and technical knowledge, physical strength has been pushed to the second position. The latest developments in satellite communication and the computerised linkage has asserted the supremacy of knowledge.

The army, the air force, the navy all depend on highly, sophisticated implements based on knowledge. The nations are heavily turning to economic supremacy that can never be gained without the knowledge of trade, marketing and production — a prerogative of knowledge alone.

Knowledge is beneficial in the progress of art, literature, science, philosophy and religion. It directs a man's actions and enables him to find the difference between right and wrong, good and bad. As somebody said, "The man who claims that he knows, knows nothing; but he who claims nothing, knows!"

Knowledge leads to unity, while ignorance leads to diversity. A good life is guided by knowledge and inspired by love. So invest in knowledge that pays the best interest. It is the powerful armour to safeguard you always. It is a strong fortress that even enemies cannot penetrate.

❖ ❖ ❖ ❖ ❖

85. My Favourite Festival

Diwali is the one single festival that is celebrated throughout India. However, the way of celebration and the religious significance attached to it varies from region to region.

Diwali, or Deepavali, literally means a row of lamps. In north India flickering lamps and explosion of fire crackers commemorate the return of Lord Rama, the Prince of Ayodhya, at the end of fourteen harrowing years of banishment from his kingdom, and victory over the demon, king Ravana.

Diwali festival is celebrated by young and old alike, by wearing of new clothes, by decorating the courtyards with rangoli designs and by festooning the whole house and its surroundings with oil lamps and candles, after offering prayers to Lakshmi, the goddess of wealth, in the evening. This is followed by distributing sweets to neighbours, relatives and friends, and lighting of fireworks.

In South India, Diwali celebrates the killing of Narakasura by Lord Krishna. In memory of this event, people south of the Vindhyas rise before sunrise and take a holy bath.

Diwali also happens to be the day when the sixth Guru of the Sikhs, Guru Hargobind, was released from the Gwalior fort by Mughal Emperor Jahangir, who was overwhelmed by the Gurus's piety and devotion to God. The Sikh community observes the day with devotion and solemnity.

The Jains celebrate the day in memory of Vardhamana (Mahavira), the twenty-fourth tirthankara, who attained nirvana on this day.

For the traders and merchants, Diwali marks the close of the business year, setting of all accounts and opening of a new account. The practitioners of Ayurveda too celebrate this day in their own way, as Dhanwantari, the father of the ancient system of medicine, was supposed to be born on this day.

The cosmopolitan character of the Diwali festival is reflected in the sheer enjoyment and friendliness in which people belonging to all walks of life indulge. Diwali festival, over the years, has become the most secular in nature. The myths that surround the festival of Diwali have one central theme common to all – the victory of good over evil.

❖ ❖ ❖ ❖ ❖

86. My Favourite Scientist

My favourite scientist over the years has been Dr. Vikram A Sarabhai. A great scientist, a brilliant administrator and many-splendoured personality, he is rememberd for various contributions to science in India.

Vikram was born in 1919, and he had his schooling in Ahmedabad. He went to St. John's College in Cambridge for higher studies. He worked on problems of nuclear physics and took the Ph.D degree of the Cambridge University with a thesis on "Cosmic Ray Investigations in Tropical Latitudes" in 1947.

Dr. Sarabhai had a keen desire to establish institutions for developing new science and advanced technology, and using them for improving the living conditions of people. On his return from the United Kingdom, he started a physical research laboratory in Ahmedabad to provide for studies in theoretical physics, radio physics and electronics. Today, it serves as a leading postgraduate study centre for physics in the country.

Between 1947 and 1955, he set up two other institutions: the Ahmedabad Textile Industry's Research Institution and the Indian Institute of Management.

Dr. Sarabhai was appointed as a member of the Atomic Energy Commission in 1961. Since then his bright career started. With his keen interest in cosmic rays and the upper atmosphere he proved beyond doubt that he possessed an extraordinary mind. The Rocket Launching Station and the Space Science and Technology Centre at Thumba near Thiruvananthapuram were the outcome of his creative efforts.

After the untimely death of Dr. Homi J. Bhabha, Dr. Vikram Sarabhai took over the chairmanship of the Atomic Energy Commission. Soon he brought the Department of Atomic Energy and Space Research Organisation into closer contact.

The Community Science Centre in Ahmedabad founded by him and his family provides laboratory, library and workshop facilities for boys and girls to learn and do experiments guided by qualified scientists.

Dr. Sarabhai was the chairman of the United Nations Conference on the Exploration and Peaceful Uses of Outer Space in 1968. He was President, 14th General Conference, International Economic Agency, Vienna, Austria, in 1970. He was the recipient of many honours, both in India and abroad.

Dr. Sarabhai passed away at Kovalam near Thiruvananthapuram on December 30, 1971.

❖ ❖ ❖ ❖ ❖

87. Electricity in Modern Life

Day and night electric current flows through electric circuits, setting factories and plants in motion, and bringing light to cities and towns.

The machines that produce electricity are called generators. A turbine spins the rotor in the middle of the generator, and thus the current is produced. The rotor is spun by a jet of water, gas or steam which hits against the blades of a big fan-like turbine. The rotor and the turbine are fitted on a common shaft.

If the turbine is spun by water we have got a hydroelectric power plant, examples of which can be found on big rivers, or on fast mountain trains.

Thermal power stations make use of steam turbines to drive the generators. There is no need for dams or rivers in this case. Instead, thermal power station need a lot of fuel, coal or oil, to boil large quantities of water in order to produce steam.

Nuclear power stations obtain steam by circulating water through the hot interior of a nuclear reactor. Ten grams of nuclear fuel gives off the same heat as a wagonful of coal.

Even sunlight can be made to work to produce electricity. Special solar batteries provide light and heating for people's homes. They also supply electricity to spaceships and satellites.

It is not always convenient to send electricity through wire circuits. Therefore, people invented various storing devices called cells and batteries. Cells of different kinds are to be found in your mechanical toys, electronic watches and transistor radios.

Modern communications and transport use electricity. Electricity is also widely used in the medical field for the cure of diseases, using modern technology in the detection of these diseases. In very hot and humid places, air-conditioners are becoming a necessity, while in very cold places, heaters are in great demand. Refrigerators not only condition the temperature but also pressure and facilitate man's food supply.

There are also chances of being electrocuted if the wires are exposed. The other problem could be short circuit which can be dangerous. But the advantages of electricity far outweigh the negative aspects.

❖ ❖ ❖ ❖ ❖

88. Srinivasa Ramanujan

Ramanujan is the wizard of mathematics and is classed along with Charles Darwin and Isaac Newton by Robert Boyle as 'The Greats'. Not only was he considered the greatest mathematician of India, but, according to Prof. J.R. Mordell, also "for formal manipulation of infinite process and an instinctive feeling for algebraic formulae, he was unrivalled since the time of Euler and Jacobi." He was the first Indian too to be FRS, with Sir C.V. Raman following six years later.

Ramanujan was born at Erode on December 22, 1887. He was a brilliant student at school, and he discovered his genius in mathematics while at middle school. He thought more than what he was taught, and jotted down his creative ideas in a notebook. His notebooks have been published in photostate form, and are justly famous for the mine of openings for research they contain.

No teacher or mathematician in India could understand him. He was quite ordinary in everything except in mathematics. Once he happened to read the book *Orders of Infinity* by Prof. Hardy of Cambridge. There was a statement about prime numbers and he had also discovered something new on primes. So he wrote a long letter to Prof. Hardy who invited him to join him in his research work. At that time Ramanujan was the first research scholar in the Universtiy of Madras, after having worked for a couple of years in Port Trust.

Ramanujan sailed to England, and spent six years in mathematical research. His contributions were of high order. He became the first Indian fellow of the Royal Society by merit.

He was a great number person. Numbers up to 10,000 were his personal friends, and the easiest way to engage him was to mention to him a number, and he would start giving all its beauties.

He fell ill, returned to India, and could not recover. He died in his thirty-second year at Chetput in Madras in 1920.

The Department of Mathematics of the Madras University is named after him. The Ramanujan prize is also awarded to a budding young mathematician of high promise.

Ramanujan was indeed one of the greatest mathematicians.

❖ ❖ ❖ ❖ ❖

89. Noise Pollution

Noise has pursued man endlessly in the Modern Age. High speed means of transportation, like cars, buses, trucks and aircraft, are a source of noise. This is increasingly difficult to control.

In modern life noise interferes with people's work and rest, reduces labour productivity, and affects the nervous system. Fighting against noise is among the most urgent problems of today.

Transport remains the biggest and the most widespread source of noise in cities, accounting for as much as 60-80 per cent of it. Noise produced by industrial enterprises makes up 20-30 per cent.

To reduce city noise, a correct town building policy is essential—in laying out streets and squares, organising traffic flows, designing special types of buildings, and setting up noise protection zones and belts. When compiling noise maps, streets may be classified according to noise levels, so that town builders can adopt different approaches to them. This will reduce the impact of noise by using special techniques of layout and development.

When new constructions are well planned, the difference in noise levels is about 30 decibels. This is quite sufficient to make a flat comfortable to live in. Town builders can also develop another method of noise control. In some cases it may be advantageous to place underground the more noisy engineer constructions, transport situations and a part of traffic. This will save the city thousands of hectares of land and relieve people from noise and congestion.

Almost all cities and towns are under noise pollution. Noises from automobiles, loudspeakers, music bands, plane take off, fine crackers bursting all add to the noise pollution in cities. Some sounds are jarring and unpleasant to the ear.

Air transport contributes maximum to noise pollution and pollution through speed is in the air medium. That is how the thundering clouds deafen people when the thunder reaches the earth. An aeroplane travelling at a speed of more than 330 metres per second, crossing the sound barrier, creates quake-like vibrations in the atmosphere, dangerous to one's eardrums.

❖ ❖ ❖ ❖ ❖

90. Punctuality

Punctuality is an essential part of our disciplined life and nature. "Unfaithfulness in the keeping of an appointment is an act of clear dishonesty. You may as well borrow a person's money as his time," points out Horace Mann.

The sun rises with seasonal punctuality and so it sets. The seasons turn in their cycles, and there again you have nature observing punctuality. The huge stars in the sky move on their course so punctually.

The singing of a nightingale, the migration of birds, the flowering of trees and bearing of fruit in their time, the fall of leaves in autumn, sprouting of new leaves in spring all teach us a lesson in punctuality. In fact, our birth, growth, decay and death are so planned by the Supreme Power that they must follow a pattern of rhythm and punctuality.

Punctuality is the soul of business. It has been called the 'politeness of princes', a badge of sincerity, discipline and success.

Men who have made punctuality their virtue take no chances in being late. If they know that a certain train or bus might make them late, they take the earlier one. They prefer to be a little early rather than be late.

People who cannot keep appointments make others miserable. Some people believe they are very smart because they always arrive late. They have no objection to being inconsiderate and even rude. At the theatre, they spoil the pleasure of others; at the dinner party they disgust their host and hostess.

There are occasions, of course, when one cannot help being late but when one can, one should remember the example of a king of England who had once been invited by a French portrait painter to visit his studio to look at some pictures. As the king could not be there at 3 o'clock, the hour of the appointment, he rushed an aide-de-camp at half past two to say that he would he there at quarter past three, and there he was on the dot!

When you have made an appointment, which is a kind of promise, be careful to keep it at the appointed time. If you must cancel an appointment, make sure to inform the person concerned as soon as possible.

"I have always been a quarter hour before my time, and it has made a man of me," said Nelson. Follow this advice and make a successful man of yourself.

Be punctual, always be on time. You expect it of others, and they expect it of you. It will pay you good dividends. By being punctual in business or meeting people at the appointed hour, you will show them your sense of time, and in turn, enjoy their respect.

❖ ❖ ❖ ❖ ❖

91. Superstitions

By and large, human beings all over the world are a superstitious lot. Frankly, there is no denying that each one of us does believe in some sort of a pet superstition — either a lucky number, a lucky day or a lucky charm.

Why speak of superstitious individuals? Even the United States navy never launched a new ship on any Friday or any 13th! Most high rise buildings in the USA do not have the thirteenth floor; after the twelfth, the next floor is fourteenth.

Of all superstitious beliefs, the fear of number 13 really takes the cake. In France, you will never find a house or a hospital bed with the number 13. Most airlines in many parts of the world omit seat number 13 on their planes.

How did this number 13 phobia begin in the first place? Some say its basis is found in Norse mythology. The Vikings were known to be terribly superstitious people, and it is said, their great warrior Balder was killed at a banquet attended by thirteen guests.

Meeting a black cat is another widely known superstition. In England a black cat crossing a person's path was always considered unlucky; in Egypt just the opposite was true. In ancient Egypt the cat was sacred to Goddess Isis, hence the belief. However, the one superstition considered lucky all over the world is that concerning the horse shoe. Finding a horse shoe is accepted all around the world as a lucky sign.

Not to stumble on the entrance or doorway is an old Roman superstition. Tiberius Gracchus, the great Roman statesman, stumbled on the doorway of his home and died on the same day.

You might have very often seen people refusing to light three cigarettes with one match. This superstition was also born in the interests of safety. For the British soldier fighting in the Boer war lighting three cigarettes was good as inviting danger. It gave the enemy sniper enough time to spot the light, take aim, and fire, killing 'the third man'.

As Bacon says, "The general root of superstition is that men observe when things hit, and not when they miss; and commit to memory the one, and forget and pass over the other."

A man should not be bound by superstitions if he wants to progress in life. Instead, he should lead others out of ignorance into the realm of belief and knowledge.

❖ ❖ ❖ ❖ ❖

92. Hockey

It is believed that hockey had its origin in Persia, in West Asia. Later it reached Western countries and slowly came back to Eastern countries many years later. A bas-relief by Themistoles uncovered in Athens many years ago, points to the prevalence of some form of game in Greece before Chirst. possibly the old Olympic and Isthumin games in Greece included it in their contests.

The Olympic Games of ancient Greece did include a game like hockey when a ball was struck with hooded sticks. The Romans who came after the Greeks bettered the game. When they went on their empire building activity, they took the game with balls to the lands which they conquered. And that is how hockey reached Britain and became the Britishers' game. Later in Ireland and Scotland, 'hurley' and 'shinty' – games like hockey – were played.

Hockey as it exists today came from Britain. It became a popular game from the middle of the nineteenth century. The first hockey club, 'Blackheath', was then formed. The rules of the game were formulated by the Wimbledon Club consisting of the people of Victorian England. These were adopted by the Hockey Association in 1886. In course of time improvements came and modern hockey was born.

When the British set up their rule in India, they brought hockey with them. Soon the Indians picked up the game and performed well in international matches and Olympics.

Between 1928 and 1956 India won six Olympic gold medals in hockey. India also set a world record in the 1932 Los Angeles Olympics unbeaten to this day — she beat the USA 24-1.

The hockey teams now consist of 11 players each. The blade of the hockey stick must not be more than two inches wide and it should not weigh over eight ounces. The white ball has the same weight and size as that of a cricket ball.

❖ ❖ ❖ ❖ ❖

93. Dr. S. Radhakrishnan

September 5 is a red-letter day. On this day, called Teachers' Day, educationists, teachers and students remember Dr. S. Radhakrishnan, who started his career as a teacher, and finally ended up as the President of India.

Dr. Sarvepalli Radhakrishnan was born on September 5, 1888, in a middle class family in the temple town of Tiruttani in Tamil Nadu. He studied in a school first at Tirupati, and then at Vellore for his undergraduate studies. Later he joined Madras Christian College, and studied philosophy. In 1909, at the age of 21, he took his MA degree with the topmost honours.

Dr. Radhakrishnan was very rich in his knowledge, but poor in his financial status, especially during his student life. It was a touching story to learn that during the middle of his educational career, he had to auction his university medals to meet his educational expenses and to support his family.

As a professor of philosophy, he excelled in the universities of Madras, Mysore, Andhra, Benaras and Calcutta. He also distinguished himself as a visiting professor to Oxford, Chicago and London University.

Dr. Radhakrishnan served as the Vice-Chancellor of Andhra University in the period 1931-36, and gave fresh boost to its development. Then as Vice-Chancellor of Benaras University he raised the standards of teaching and improved the finances. In 1936 he was invited to fill the chair of the Spalding Professor of Eastern Religions and Ethics of Oxford, and retained it for 16 years with distinction.

Dr. Radhakrishnan was a great scholar in both the Eastern and Western philosophies. He lectured to learned and respectable Western academic audiences to interpret the East to the West in most persuasive words. He was India's cultural ambasaador without an equal.

At the age of 61, he was the Vice-President of India. On May 12, 1962, after Dr. Rajendra Prasad, he was elected the President of India. Some of his advisors requested him that they might be permitted to celebrate September 5 as his birthday. He told them to celebrate it as 'Teachers' Day in the country. It reflects how much importance he gave to the teaching profession—the noblest profession since the olden days.

Indians from all walks of life should emulate Dr. Radhakrishnan, a man of letters with principles, who devoted his life to the service of the nation with single-mindedness. He said, "Until and unless we have dedicated and committed teachers who take to teaching as a mission in their lives, we cannot have a good educational system." He died on April 17, 1975 at Chennai. His books are widely read.

❖ ❖ ❖ ❖ ❖

94. Life of an Indian Farmer

Let us never forget that the cultivation of the earth is the most important labour of man. When tillage begins, other arts follow. The farmers, therefore, are the founders of civilisation.

Indian is largely an agricultural country, and the farmer here is the backbone of the Indian society. He is the real father of the nation, as he is the one who is responsible for our sustenance on this earth.

An India farmer depicts a picture of honesty, hard work, suffering and poverty. In spite of having modern amenities like tractors, threshers and electricity, the average farmer works with his old, rough tools. He ploughs his fields with a wooden plough drawn by a team of oxen. He toils in the scorching heat of the summer sun, or in the biting cold of the winter months.

A farmer's life is not an easy one. He has to work very hard to enjoy the yield of his field. His work commences early in the morning when he takes his oxen to the fields. He ploughs the fields, sows seeds and waters the crops. He has to take a lot of precautions against the menace of rats, stray cattle, wild animals, birds, and so on.

The farmer leads a very simple life eating simple food and wearing coarse cotton clothes. He follows traditions, customs and superstitions. His cattle are his most valuable assets, and he takes a lot of care of them.

The farmer is dependent to a larger extent on rains so that he does not have to unnecessarily spend on irrigating his fields. Being rather poor, he can ill-afford to spend money on unnecessary luxuries. He has to spend on manure, chemical fertilisers and water, and also on good seeds that will bring him a good yield.

The farmer may be uneducated, but he is always honest and hardworking. He is always hospitable. Now voluntary non-government organisations are coming forward to educate farmers in various way. The state governments are also encouraging them for better production by giving them loans on easy terms for the investment in modern methods of farming, like tubewells, pumpsets, tractors, sprinklers, water storage tanks and other farm implements. With such facilities being available to them, the lot of the farmer should become easier with better living conditions.

❖ ❖ ❖ ❖ ❖

93. My Hobby

Hobbies are the leisure-time interests of individuals. The pursuit of a hobby offers enjoyment, education, companionship with others of similar interests, relaxing diversion, and very often monetary gains.

My favourite hobby is stamp collecting. From a mania in the 1840's, stamp collecting has grown into one of the world's most popular hobbies, a science and a business activity today.

Stamp collecting began immediately after the world saw the first postage stamp in 1840 issued by Great Britain. The bits of coloured paper were a curiosity and used specimens were retained by some people. When other countries followed Britain, the idea of exchanging stamps came into existence, and collecting became more interesting. Thus the hobby was born. The collection and study of postage stamps is known as philately.

The nature of collections varies from person to person. One may collect all the stamps one can lay one's hands on. My sources of stamps are letters coming to my father and two elder brothers, their offices, my neighbours and friends. Some collectors concentrate on a specialised branch like stamps of a continent, a country, or a theme such as animals, sports or space. There are certain well to do collectors whose interest is confined to 'mint' or unused stamps. Some people take a fancy to collecting First Day Covers. I generally have all of these since my collection is at present very limited. Whatever be the field of specialisation, a genuine interest in the hobby, spare time, good contacts, and willingness and ability to spend some money are the prerequisites of a good collection.

What makes a stamp precious is variety, demand and good condition. There are many philatelic gems which are much sought after. I have in my collection a stamp with the picture of Sher Shah Suri, priced at 20 naye paise, which the government released to honour the memory of this great ruler. Sher Shah Suri had many achievements to his credit. He gave a new vigour and trend to the early Indian postal system between 1540 and 1545. The design of the stamp is vertical and rectangular.

I also have a couple of stamps with errors in printing, and so this has a high value among stamps. I have more than a thousand stamps in my collection.

❖ ❖ ❖ ❖ ❖

96. Importance of Trees

Trees are the lifeline of a crowded urban region. Their importance to humankind cannot be weighed in terms of mere words. They give us fresh air (oxygen) to breathe. They are instrumental in bringing rain by causing clouds to form. They prevent floods from occurring by helping the soil to absorb heavy rainfall. They provide coolness through the shade of their leaves.

Trees stabilise the soil, protecting the many forms of life in it. They prevent soil erosion through their roots which hold the soil together. They fertilise the soil with their dead leaves which contain the minerals that all creatures need for their growth.

Trees surround us with beauty through their variety in shape, height, colour and flowers. They provide the fuel we use for cooking, such as firewood and charcoal. They provide us building material for houses, doors, windows and furniture.

Artists use the wood of the trees to carve statues and various works of art. They provide raw material needed to make paper for the books, newspapers and magazines we read.

Trees provide seeds and fruits to eat. They provide wood for the coffins in which human beings make their last journey. Trees connect heaven and earth. With their roots deeply entrenched in the earth and their boughs with their leaves stretched to their creator, they continually glorify God and offer Him thanks. God provides for us continuously through the presence of trees.

Trees have many medicinal uses. The leaves of the neem are known to cure many an ailment. Many berries and fruits yield oils that are used in the preparation of medicines. The bark of some trees, like cinchona, are also used for remedial purposes.

Government recommends every citizen to plant at least one tree in his lifetime.

❖ ❖ ❖ ❖ ❖

97. Growing Violence in the World

Today, the world is strife-town and plagued with violence. It has been a witness to clashes and violence all over the world. Violence, terrorism and fanatism have caused untold miseries to the innocent people who have unfairly became victims at their hands. It is indeed distressing to hear or read about such cases, not only at homes, but also at educational institutions, markets, workplaces, tourist spots and so on.

All countries have their own problems that are compounded by sudden spurts of violence in various pockets of their country. Citizens go on strike when their demands are not met, and sometimes these take an ugly turn, and violence in the form of clashes among the striking workers and management can become destructive. There is distruction of public property, likes buses being burnt, breaking of furniture, windows, doors, looting, not sparing people around, etc.

Many people holding high posts are often threatened by these irate workers, and they are sometimes fearful of harm to their families. Protection is not possible for all the people all the time, and hence a sense of insecurity haunts them. There is no doubt that such eruptions of violence only drains the country of its financial resources.

Youth are generally the ones to be instigated by those with vested interests in creating havoc and anarchy among the people. The rush of young blood is fully exploited by them, and these gullible scapegoats resort to violence.

Women and children too are not spared. One hears of cases of bride burning due to lack of provision of dowry by her parents. Female foeticide is another cruelty practised in many areas.

Though the world is becoming more and more progressive, we see side by side the growing trend of violence. Nation versus nation, state versus state, man versus man — the World becomes a place of greed and insatiety, leaving behind a trail of devastation, hunger, death, homelessness, etc.

We have to make joint efforts to make peace a possibility on this earth. It is for us to make the effort. The result is always in God's hands, as Gandhiji once said.

98. Untouchability

Untouchability has been the bane of the Indian social fabric. But for long years we have been blessed to have people like Gandhiji, Ambedkar, Bal Gangadhar Tilak, Raja Rammohan Roy, Dayananda Saraswati, Rabindranath Tagore and such other stalwarts who dedicated their lives to remove this social evil that was a blot on the Indian culture.

Casteism has been existing in India for centuries, which has been eroding, our secular values. In olden days whey kings ruled the country, some enjoyed the status of being favoured by these kings while others were relegated to carry out menial jobs.

Now that India has attained independence and is proclaimed to be a secular and democratic country, the question of servility and untouchability does not arise. Thanks to people like Mahatma Gandhi, people have now started actively to remove this social stigma. A lot more needs to be done to eradicate this corrupt practice.

India is a land of villages, and there are still many such villages where untouchability is still in practice. The villagers need to be educated about the equality of all beings on this earth. Many non-government organisations are actively involved in this direction. In rural areas of the country, the caste system is so dominant that it has affected the social fabric of the society. In many villages, it has resulted in mass migration to cities. But there too it persists in the slums that surround the big cities.

In certain areas of the country, where backwardness still prevails, untouchability has resulted in great violence. If a person from a lower caste has violated a rule set down by the sarpanch of that village, then there is heavy punishment for the individual. This leads to clashes among the untouchables and the rest of the villagers, resulting in deaths of many members of the scheduled castes and burning of their property.

There are still miles to go before we see satisfactory results. True emancipation will come only when poverty and ignorance are eliminated from the face of the country.

❖ ❖ ❖ ❖ ❖

99. A Stitch in Time Saves Nine

Shakespeare said, "Make use of time, let not advantage slip." This highly didactic dictate applies in every field of our activity today. There is a time and place for everything. You must know the true value of time; snatch, seize and enjoy every moment of it. No idleness, no laziness, no procrastination. Never put off till tomorrow what you can do today.

If work is done in time, it saves a lot of labour later on. For example, you notice that the button on your short is hanging loose. It would be better to sew it on tightly before you lose the button altogether.

This applies to studies also. If you keep studying daily and not putting it off to a later date, examination time would not be one of tension and worry. Otherwise your mind will not be able to cope up with all the last minute cramming and learning. Everything will seem to be new and Greek to you then.

Don't procrastinate and defer discussions to a later time. Do it now. The present is the time for action. If you have to send a reply to a letter, why postpone doing it when a later date would not have the same impact that an immediate response has? Making excuses later on may not be the solution to patch up hurt feelings.

As far as friendship is concerned, the right act at the opportune time binds friendships. If you need to apologise to someone, do it at once so that no ill feelings linger.

Where health is concerned, never neglect is by postponing taking proper medication. If, for instance, there is a wound on your foot, take proper precautions to treat it before it becomes septic. The key word here is now, not later.

When you find some task unpleasant, there is a tendency to postpone doing it. You know it has to be done, so why let it obsess your mind by not completing it? Think of the relief and peace of mind you will get when it is over and done with.

So, remember, do what has to be done, now. This will surely give you a lot of mental satisfaction. Never put off for tomorrow what you can do today. Take care of your things, and act in time before it is too late.

❖ ❖ ❖ ❖ ❖

LETTERS

1. The Basics

Broadly speaking, letters can be classified as informal or formal.

Informal Letters

Any letter written to a friend or a member of a family is known as an informal or private letter. It can be informal or social.

Formal Letters

Formal letters are again classified into official and business letters.

Business letters are formal but form the bulk of letters written in the world.

Official letters are more formal than the business letters.

A formal letter is written between two organisations, or between an individual and an organisation.

❖ ❖ ❖ ❖ ❖

2. Informal Letters

All letters have to follow six guidelines which are given below:

1. The name and address of the writer at the top right-hand side, followed by the date below.
2. Next comes the greeting or salutation on the left-hand side of the page, followed by a comma.
3. The body of the letter in which you want to write what you want to convey.
4. The conclusion which is usually in the form of communicating your fondness or affection for the person you are writing to.
5. Your signature.
6. Superscription or address on the envelope to whom the letter is being sent.

Example

'Bajpai House'
2, Golf Links
Hyderabad – 500001
June 10, 2005

My dear Madhav,

I was very happy ....

....

....

Yours affectionately,
Rahul.

Informal letters can be private or social. Private letters are between friends, relatives, teachers and pupils, etc. These include friendly letters, including private, personal and descriptive letters.

Forms of Salutation and Superscription

Addresses	Solutation	Superscription
1. Elders	My dear Father	Yours affectionately,
	or Mother	or
	Dear Brother / Sister / Uncle / Aunt, etc.	Your loving son or affectionate brother / niece, etc.
Youngsters	My dear/Ram, Dear/Ram,	Your affectionate, father, uncle, etc.
2. Friends	My dear/Ram, Dear/Ram,	Yours sincerely or Yours very sincerely or Yours affectionately or Sincerely yours or Yours ever
3. Acquaintances	Dear/Mr. Ram, Dear/Miss Sharma,	Yours sincerely or Yours truly or
4. Strangers	Sir, Dear Sir, Dear Madam,	Yours very truly
5. Teachers, Professors and Principals	Sir, Dear Sir, Dear Madam, Respected Sir,	Yours most obediently, Yours obediently, Yours sincerely
6. Businessmen	Sir/s,	Yours faithfully,

Addresses	Solutation	Superscription
Firms	Dear Sir, Dear Madam,	
Application for appointment	Sir,	Yours faithfully,
7. Newspaper Editor	Sir,	Yours faithfully, Yours etc.
8. Complaints and requests of officials From one officer to another	Sir, Dear Sir,	Yours faithfully,

Examples of Private Letters

1. **Write a letter to your father requesting him to allow you to visit a few historical places outside the town, and to send you money for that.**

102, Lal Bagh Road
Bangalore
May 20, 2005

My dear father,

Our school is going on an educational tour to Delhi, Agra, Mathura and Jaipur in October. It is a golden opportunity for me to learn about the culture, architecture and sculpture of these places. I have also been wanting to see the Taj Mahal for long. I hope you will allow me to go on this tour.

I need Rs. 1,000 for the trip. Whatever balance is there will be adjusted against the hostel fee for the month of October-November. I hope this will not be a great sum for you to send me.

Please give my love and regards to Mother, and love to Amrita.

Your loving son,
Raghav.

2. Write a letter to your friend congratulating him on his success in the Board exams.

19, Prithvi Road,
Palace Layout,
Jaipur
May 30, 2005

My dear Ashwin,

Thank you very much for your letter. First of all, let me congratulate you on your brilliant performance! Your parents must be proud to hear that you have scored cent per cent in mathematics! Naturally, with over 95 per cent average; you will surely get admission into the college of your choice. My very best wishes to you for that!

I shall see you soon when I come there with my aunt and uncle next month.

I wish you all the best for the future.

Yours lovingly,
Nitesh

3. Write a letter to your uncle thanking him for the cash gift sent by him on your birthday.

25, Landsdown View,
Gandhi Nagar,
Vadodara
18, February 2005

Dear Uncle,

It was very nice of you to have remembered my birthday and sent me a considerable amount as gift. I have been wanting to buy some educational books which will be useful to me as reference material. I am also planning to get reference CD's that have recently come into the market, and are quite cheap.

Thank you so much, once again, dear Uncle, for your generosity. I will always remember this kind gesture on your part.

Please convey my thanks and regards to Aunty, and love to Mukund and Mamata.

Yours affectionately
Ajay

4. Write a condolence letter to your teacher, expressing your sympathies on the expiry of her father.

25/2, Trinity Meadows,
Residency Park,
Bangalore–90
15, September 2005

My dear Madam,

I write this letter to express my condolence at the expiry of your dear father. It would indeed be a blow to yourself and other members in the family.

I pray to God that he would give you the needed consolation and comfort to put up with this great personal loss.

But I am sure you would overcome this tragedy very fast because you are a strong-willed person. And I am proud of you on account of this disposition.

With respects,

Yours truly
Sheena

5. Write a letter to your mother informing her that you are coming home for vacations.

G A-13, Rohini Apts.
Ambuja Nagar,
Ranchi–12
3 March, 2005

My dear Mother,

Hope this finds all of you at home in the best of health.

You will be glad to know that our school will be closing for summer vacations from the 30th of this month.

I shall be leaving this place with Shlok and Sachin in the school bus on 29th night and be there early the next morning.

I hope you and Papa are keeping fine. Love to Nikhil.

Your loving son,
Nilesh

6. **Write a letter to your grandparents asking them to come and spend a few days with you.**

232, Gandhi Marg,
Pantnagar,
Allahabad,
16, April 2005

Dear Grandma and Grandpa

My summer holidays have commenced since yesterday. This year I have joined the Cricket Coaching camp which starts on the 20th. It will last for two months, and hence I will not be able to come to Mumbai this year.

Instead, why don't you both come here for a change? It has been so long since you came this side. Please come and stay with us for at least a month so that we can plan a week's holiday at Kalimpong which is such a pretty place.

If you let me know the details of the train and coach and seat number, and date of arrival here, I shall come to the station with Papa to receive you both.

I have so much to tell you.

Eagerly looking forward to your arrival!

With love,

Your grandson,
Zubin

7. **Write a letter to your friend who has met with an accident.**

24-A, Rockhill Road,
Fort,
Trichy–10
22, October, 2005

My dear Rajini,

Your cousin told me yesterday that you fell down the stairs in your school and have fractured your leg. It came as such a shock to me. It must be very painful, and I hope you are taking a much-needed rest.

I wish I had holidays now so that I could come and visit you, and be of some cheer to you. I am sending you some story books which will help you to pass the time. I am also sending you two audio cassettes which I hope you will like listening to.

Please take care and get well soon.

Yours affectionately
Niharika

8. Write a letter to your sister telling her how you spent your summer vacation.

12/31, Santosh Nagar
Hyderabad
29, June 2005

Dear Sharmila

As you know, I had gone to Srinagar, Pahalgam and Gulmarg with the Datta family. First we flew to Delhi and halted for a night at Grandpa's house. Next morning we flew to Srinagar, and stayed at the Tourist Centre. Kirti, Disha and I shared a room with Mrs. Datta, The boys and Mr. Datta shared the other room. We went boating on Dal Lake, visited the Shankaracharya Temple and the Nishat Garden. Next day we went to Gulmarg by buas and stayed there overnight. We went to Khilanmarg and took the winch up the mountain. We used the sleds also to slide down the slopes.

Next morning we went to Pahalgam and did a lot of trekking alongside the river. It was full of fun. We returned to Srinagar the following day. We ate a lot of fruits and nuts. These places are worth visiting as they are like paradise. You must visit them with your family soon.

Please convey my love to Jeejaji, Bunty and Pinky.

Yours affectionately
Neeta

9. Write a letter to your younger brother advising him against mixing with bad boys.

20, Navinagar Complex
Budhwara
Ludhiana – 2
May 20, 2005

My dear Piyush,

I was shocked to receive a letter from your principal. He had enclosed your marks card for the first term of college and it is painful to see you scoring so low marks, all below 50 per cent. The Principal has remarked that you are in had company and have been punished on several occasions for your bad behaviour.

You must remember that your purpose in college is to study well, be on your best behaviour and learn the value of discipline and good conduct.

Soon you will have to think of higher studies or start a career, neither of which is possible if you neglect your studies. Please pay proper attention to your studies. You should realise what our parents are expecting of us. They have sacrificed everything so that we both can do well in studies and get jobs to support them as they grow older.

I hope you will mend your ways and show better performance this year.

Your loving brother,
Mohan

10. Write a letter of thanks to your friend who has congratulated you on your brilliant success in the Board Examination.

2/A, Raheja Towers
Museum Road,
Bangalore–2
5 July 2005

My dear Rashmi,

Thanks so much for your congratulatory letter on my success in the Board Examination.

I must tell you that your mother's advice of waking up early and putting in two hours of study has been the secret of my success. Indeed, I found that I could retain much more in my memory studying in the early hours. This has helped me a lot during my revision of lessons.

Since she has advised you also to do likewise, I am sure you are following her advice seriously. Now it will be your turn to appear for the Board Examination next year. Do act upon it.

Wishing you the same success, and thanking you once again for your kind letter.

Yours sincerely,
Mahima

11. Write a letter to your cousin apologising for hurting her feelings with your rude reply.

31, Sonali Apts.
Besant Nagar
Chennai–90

My dear Sonam,

I know you must be very angry and hurt by my rude behaviour. I am really sorry for what I said yesterday to you in a fit of anger. Please do accept my humble apologies.

Believe me, what I did was absolutely wrong, and I realise it now. But at that moment. I was blind and deaf to all reasoning. Nitin had scolded me just 10 minutes earlier over this sensitive issue. Your advice added fuel to the fire, as I felt right then that you were all unnecessarily interfering in my affairs, but now I see that what you both told me was rational and sensible. I have now decided to follow your advice, and keep away from this issue and not get myself involved in it.

Thank you very much for your advice and once again, please forgive me for my unruly behaviour.

Yours sincerely,
Aditi

12. Write a letter to your friend describing her about your visit to a book fair.

24, Madhuban Complex
Rohini
New Delhi
10 February, 2005

My Dear Girija,

Last Sunday I had gone to the World Book Fair at Pragati Maidan. This is held once in four years, and lasts for about 10 to 14 days. Various countries participate in this grand fair, and publishers from all over the country too have their stalls. Various buildings have these books, and the biggest hall in the centre of the Maidan had the international section.

It is very difficult to visit all the stalls in a day, and so I went to a select few only. There were books on science, commerce, general knowledge, philosophy, religion, cookery, arts, comics, health, novels, etc.

I was overjoyed to find among them some rare books which I immediately purchased. One of the stalls in the international section was offering a set of encyclopedias of 20 volumes for Rs. 15,000. I booked the set and offered to buy it from them the following day.

Today, I am the proud owner of these valuable books, and they adorn the topmost rack of my bookshelf in my room. My father has told me to take good care of them. He too has started browsing through the first volume!

Convey my best regards to your parents.

Yours sincerely,
Lata

13. Write a letter of consolation to your cousin who has failed in an examination.

1539, Maruti Towers
Nazarabad
Bhopal
June 25, 2005

My dear Mridula,

I was sad to hear that you could not clear the examination. I sincerely sympathise with your bad luck. Don't forget that success and failure go hand in hand. Please take heart and do not give way to grief.

You are fortunate that this is not a Board examination or a final examination, but just a term examination. You still have time to study very hard and make up for the loss. You must put in a lot of effort and seek help from your teachers if you don't understand something. Don't give in to despair, but from now on work with determination to show that you can be as good as the others. So cheer up, and all the best!

Yours sincerely,
Malvika

14. Write a letter to a friend telling him what you intend to do after your examination.

3, Temple Road,
Shastrinagar,
Varanasi
20, April 2005

My dear Rohit,

You have asked me in your letter my future plans after the Board examination.

At first, all that I want to do is relax for 10 days! I want to catch up with my hobby of stamp collecting. I would like to watch a couple of good movies on television. Then I would like to visit a few friends.

As regards my future, I want to go in for medicine. Both my parents are doctors, and my brother is already studying medicine. So I am also inspired to become one. So I would like to spend a lot of time preparing for the various entrance exams. I have my family members to help me with the preparations, and am also planning to join the Brilliant Group for coaching.

Write to me and let me know what your plans are.

Yours sincerely,
Jatin

15. Write a letter to your father requesting him to attend the Annual Day at your school.

15, JLB Road,
Gandhinagar
Ahmedabad
18, April 2005

My dear Papa,

Our school exams are over, and the annual day function will be held on 30 April. Would you, Mama and Ankita attend the function which begins at 2 p.m.? The function will get over at 6 p.m.

I am taking part in a drama and group singing. After the variety entertainment there will be prize distribution. The Chief Guest will be the Governor of Gujarat. I will be receiving five prizes. You will be getting the invitation tomorrow. So please do come. After the function, you can take me home for the vacations.

With love,

Yours lovingly,
Naren

16. Write a letter to your father in United States, giving him some happy news.

19, Gold Links Road,
Azadpur Colony
Shimla
June 29, 2005

My dear Papa,

We all miss you a lot here, but happy to hear that you will be coming to visit us soon.

Papa, you will be very happy and proud to hear that I have been selected for admission into Maulana Azad Medical College in Delhi. I received the letter informing me about this just yesterday.

I wish you had been here to celebrate with me this proud moment. Don't forget to reward me for this achievement!

With regards and best wishes from all of us.

Yours affectionately,
Sapna

Examples of Social Letters

1. Write a letter to your friend congratulating her on her engagement.

15, Tank Bund Road,
Hyderabad
16, August 2005

Dear Priya,

I am so happy to hear that you got engaged yesterday to Bhaskar.

I have known Bhaskar since my childhood days. We used to play together till he went to Nainital to be in boarding school. But we used to catch up with all that he missed when he used to come home for vacations.

I always used to tease him that he would marry a fat person like me finally, because he always used to tease me about my being fat. I am very glad for him though that he got such a beautiful and slim girl like you to be his life partner, I wish you both all the best. My parents join me in wishing you all the best in life.

Don't forget to invite me to your wedding!

Your loving friend,
Madhumita

2. Write a letter to your sister on getting a good job.

115, MG Road,
CIS Colony
Nagpur
5 January 2005

My dear Chandra,

Happy New Year to you! And also my heartiest congratulations to you on getting such a prestigious job in Infosys.

Neha told me that there was stiff competition for this post, so it is all the more creditable for you to have secured it.

I know your capabilities and intelligence. I am sure you will soon forge ahead and make your mark in this reputable company. We all wish you the very best. Mysore is a good place to reside and work in, and I have seen the Infosys complex there. Beautiful is not just the word for it — it is heaven to work there!

With best wishes,

Yours affectionately,
Chitra

3. Write a letter to your cousin on winning the elections at her college.

990, Hailey Road,
Kanchan Bagh
Agra

3, October 2005

My dear Shweta,

Heartiest congratulations on winning the elections in your university and being elected as the Secretary of the Students Body. You will now become extremely busy, not only with your studies, but also with steering the student wing of the university. We all wish you luck and smooth sailing.

With best wishes,

Yours sincerely,
Salina

4. Write a letter to your friend inviting him to dinner.

3, Cariappa Circle
Anand Vihar,
Rajkot
15, December 2005

My dear Nikhil,

My grandfather is completing 80 years on 20 December. We are holding a dinner party in his honour at our house on that day. It is a small gathering, and he has specially asked that you too be invited as he is very fond of you.

Please do join at 8 p.m. And no presents please!

Yours sincerely,
Pranav

5. Write a letter accepting the invitation.

25, Madangir Street,
JB Singh Colony
Rajkot
17, December 2005

My dear Pranav,

Thank you very much for inviting me to the dinner on 20 December. I feel so honoured to be included by your grandfather amongst the invitees.

I shall be delighted to attend the dinner at 8 pm.

Thanking you,

Yours sincerely,
Nikhil

6. Write a letter declining the invitation

25, Madangir Street,
JB Singh Colony
Rajkot
17, December 2005

My dear Pranav,

Thank you so much for your kind invitation. I feel highly honoured to be among the special invitees. It is very kind of your grandfather to specially extend an invitation to me for dinner on his birthday.

I am sorry to inform you that I will not be able to attend the dinner as I going to Udaipur tomorrow to attend the funeral rites of my uncle. I will be returning only after a fortnight. But please convey my best wishes and thanks to your grandfather. I shall pray for his continued health.

Yours sincerely,
Nikhil

7. Send an invitation to a banquet to your friend.

Mr. Jacob Thomas requests the pleasure of your company at the banquet at Ashoka Hall, Hotel Maurya Sheraton, on Sunday, December 10, 2004 at 1 pm.

282, Shreyus,
Chennai
December 3, 2004.

8. Write a letter accepting the invitation

Mr. Andrew Gales is glad to accept the invitation to the banquet on Sunday, December 10, 2004. It would be a great pleasure to meet old friends at the gathering.

15, Anna Nagar,

Chennai

December 5, 2004.

9. Send a letter declining the invitation

Mr. Andrew Gales presents his compliments to Mr. Jacob Thomas and thanks him for this kind invitation, but regrets his inability to attend the banquet on Sunday, December 10, 2004.

15, Anna Nagar,

Chennai

December 5, 2004.

10. Send an invitation letter to your friend for a birthday party.

Mr. and Mrs. Sharma

request

the pleasure of your company

on the first birthday of their son

on Sunday, June, 9, 2004 at 5 pm

at their residence

24, Mawbrey's Road, Chennai-2.

11. Send an invitation to your friend to attend your wedding.

Smt. and Shri Narayan Shastri

request the pleasure of the company of

....

on the auspicious occasion of the

wedding of their daughter

POOJA

with

ANAND SHASTRI

(Son of Smt. & Shri Prabhu Shastri)

at 301, Dilshad Garden, New Delhi

on Sunday, June 23, 2005

RSVP

Family and Friends

12. Send an invitation to attend an inauguration

KESHAV BROTHERS

request the pleasure of your company

on the occasion of the

INAUGURATION

of their New Departmental Stores

SHOPPERS' STOP

at

3rd Cross, Koramangala, Bangalore-21

on Friday, January 10, 2005 at 10 am.

With best compliments from

Barton & Sons, MG Road

Bangalore-1.

13. Formal acceptance of the invitation

Mr. and Mrs. Bandharkar accept with great pleasure Keshav Brothers invitation to attend the inauguration of the new Departmental Stores, Shopper's Stop on Friday, January 10, 2005 at 10 am.

21, 15th Main Jayanagar 8th Block

Bangalore

January 5, 2005.

14. Informal acceptance of the invitation.

21, 15th Main,

Jayanagar 8th Block,

Bangalore

January 5, 2005.

Dear Dheeraj Keshav

Thanks for your invitation to the inauguration of your new Departmental Store, Shopper's Stop, on January 10, 2005 at 10 am. We will both definitely attend the function and be there on time.

Yours sincerely,

Deep Bandharkar

15. Informal rejection of the invitation.

21, 15th Main,
Jayanagar 8th Block,
Bangalore
January 5, 2005

Dear Dheeraj,

We regret our inability to accept your invitation to the inauguration of your new Departmental Store, Shoppers' Stop, on January 10, 2005, as we will not be in station.

Your sincerely,
Deep Bhandarkar

16.Send a letter to your friend, thanking her for the wedding present.

2. Napean Sea Road,
Mumbai
June 10, 2005

Dear Pratima,

Thank you so much for the lovely kitchen set that you have sent all the way from the USA! They are perfect to start setting up our house. Mahesh joins me in thanking you for the same.

Thank you once again, and with love from both of us.

Yours affectionately
Gita

17.Send a letter to your friend thanking him for his hospitality.

15, Chambers Road,
R.K. Puram
Cuttack

Dear Arvind,

First I would like to thank you, Nisha and the children for your great hospitality, and for making our two-day stay with you so wonderful.

You took time off from your work to accompany us to the various places and to help us in our purchases for the wedding.

You must all surely come for Divya's wedding and be with us well ahead of the marriage commencement. I shall be sending you the invitations in another ten days.

Thanking you once again,

Yours affectionately,
Rakesh

18. Send a condolence letter to a friend who has lost his young brother.

20, Anie Besant Road,
Ganganagar,
Chennai
20 May 2005

Dear Ravi,

I was shocked to hear about the death of your 10-year-old brother in the bus accident. I feel deeply grieved, and I am at a loss how to console you. Just yesterday he was talking to me over the phone saying that he had won first prize for recitation competition in his class.

Nothing that I can write can be of much consolation. Only time can heal such deep wounds. I shall try to be there next week and be with you for a week.

With full sympathies,

Yours,
Naresh

19. Acknowledgement of sympathy

15, Cunningham Road,
Bangalore
24, May 2005

My dear Naresh,

I thank you for your letter expressing grief over Babu's untimely death. It is so sad that due to no fault of his he had to be run over by a bus. But these are the ways of God, and we must accept His wise ways. The only consolation it's that my dear brother is with his Maker.

I am looking forward to your arrival here, as I feel you are the best person who can understand my grief best.

Yours sincerely,
Ravi

20. Intimation of funeral

15, Charing Cross
Ooty – 1
15 June, 2005

Dear Mohan,

My father, Daniel Baker, will have his funeral rites at St. Stephens Church, on 20 June, 2005, at 10 am and he will be later buried at the Ooty Cemetery at 12 moon.

Yours faithfully,
Brian Baker

3. Formal Letters — Business

Examples of Business Letters

1. MODERN HITECH EQUIPMENTS
   Tel: 26606616 Fax: 26606828

90 Leo Estate
Pallikarni.
Chennai 601302
15 June 2005

Our ref: MEQ-1/302/01
M/S JSL Towers
MG Road
Bangalore 560001

Dear Sirs,

Aluminium Ladders – Catalogue

We understand that you are a leading manufacturer of aluminium ladders.

Kindly send a copy of your latest catalogue of domestic and industrial aluminium ladders along with your price list for wholesale purchase.

As we have not done any business with you previously, please tell us about your supply terms such as whether you require advance payment or you would send the dispatch documents through the bank, etc.

Incidentally, we deal with laboratory instruments, glasswares, etc. of high quality. If we could be of any service to you, we shall welcome your enquiries.

Assuring you of our best attention on all matters.

Yours faithfully,
Sd/-
Manager (Mktg.)
for Modern Hitech

2. Write a letter to Messrs Arctic Coolers, New Delhi, complaining about a desert cooler you bought from them three months ago.

TN Narsimha

24, Prithvi Road,
New Delhi
July 24, 2005

Messr's Arctic Coolers,
Cannaught Place
New Delhi

Dear Sirs,

I purchased a desert cooler from your dealer in March during the off-season concession period. A guarantee of one year was given by your dealer, Messrs Rohit and Company, Jor Bagh. The cooler went out of order in the month of June. I contacted the dealer on phone. They promised to change or repair it within two days. So far no one has turned up in spite of repeated reminders and personal visits.

I have been compelled to write to you. A photostat copy of the sales receipt and one of the guarantee card is enclosed. If the cooler is not changed within two days, I will have to take the case to the consumer's forum.

Yours faithfully,
K.N. Narsimha

3. Enquiry about Price of Sugar

5, Chandanwari,
Bhubaneshwar
2, August 2005

Messer's Chand & Sons,
Clock Tower Circle,
Vishakapatnam

Dear Sirs,

Kindly let us know at what price per quintal, and upon what conditions of payment you are able to deliver quantities of best refined sugar.

If your price is suitable, we propose to cover all our requirements for the winter through you.

Thanking you,

Yours faithfully,

----

4. Offer of stationery

Manjunath Trading Co.
156, Kushal Bagh
Ajmer
5, October 2005

Messr's Laurie Brothers
2, Lalbagh Road,
Bangalore

Dear Sirs,

We are taking the liberty of enclosing a price list of our stationery. We hear you are interested in making large bulk purchases. We shall be pleased to send you samples of the various qualities at your convenience.

You will observe that the prices quoted are exceptionally low, and as the price of paper is expected to rise in the near future, we hope that you will place your orders as early as possible.

Yours faithfully,

----

5. Quotation for shoes

Amar Shoe Manufacturing Co.
Kanpur

10, August 2005

M/S Showorld
Sector 17,
Chandigarh

Sir,

We thank you for your letter enquiring about the prices of shoes. We are furnishing below the details

School shoes		*Rs.*	*350/- per pair*
Gent's shoes	*(1)*	*Rs.*	*750/- per pair*
	(2)	*Rs.*	*925 /- per pair*
	(3)	*Rs.*	*575/- per pair*
Ladies shoes –	*Black*	*Rs.*	*420/- per pair*
	Blue	*Rs.*	*525/- per pair*
	Grey	*Rs.*	*375/- per pair*
	White	*Rs.*	*400/- per pair*

We shall have a special trade discount of 20% on the purchases only till 15 October, after which the discount will be only 10%.

We hope you will place your order with us.

Yours faithfully,

----

6. Public Tender

Sealed tenders are invited by Bajaj and Sons for the following items which are lying in the godown of Shipping Corporation, Vishakhapatnam.

Items

1. *3 Maruti Cars 2001 – Good condition, mileage – 32,000 km.*
2. *5 Kelvinator Refrigerators — 165, all white, in perfect running condition.*
3. *2 computer tables made of compressed wood.*
4. *4 LG television (colour) sets*

Tender forms may be collected from the office of the Shipping Corporation between 4 and 5 pm. on any working day.

Separate tender form for each item together with cash Rs. 5,000/- each for the first two items, and Rs. 700/- for the other two should be submitted before the closing hours of the office on 10th May.

Tenders will be opened in the presence of the public on the same day at 1 pm.

Goods will have to be removed from the godown before 5 pm on the same day after paying the balance money in cash or by bank draft. Cheques will not be accepted.

Payment will be refunded for unaccepted tenders on 21st and 22nd October between 10 am and 12 noon.

Sd/-

Manager (Stores)

7. Letter of inquiry

Suraj Antique Dealers
15, Sonepet Marg
Ambala
15, October 2005

Dinakar Exports Co. Ltd.
Santa Cruz
Mumbai

Dear Sirs,

Mr. Mehta, the Trade Commissioner of India, informs us that you are one of the largest exporters in India. He has also sent us your catalogues. Every month we import as much as 20 pieces of antiques from Indian merchants of Mumbai. We are always short of requirements.

We shall be glad if you would supply us at least 50 pieces.

We shall refer you for information respecting our business integrity and financial position to the following firm with whom we had business relations for over ten years.

Yours faithfully,

----

8. Asking for insurance proposal form

Arhant Kirmani,
34, Pant Nagar,
New Delhi,
20 April 2005

The Manager
Life Insurance Corporation of India
Daryaganj, New Delhi

Dear Sir,

I am interested in getting myself insured for life. I shall be grateful if you would send me the necessary proposal form. If necessary please direct your agent to visit my place, and guid me in filling up the form, and oblige.

Thanking you,

Yours faithfully,

----

9. Opening a Savings Bank Account

The Manager
Indian Bank
Woods Road
Dalhousie

Dear Sir,

As I intend to open a Savings Bank Account with you, I request you to send me the necessary forms for specimen signatures.

Thanking you,

Yours faithfully,

----

10. Applying to the Post Office for VP Journal.

THOMAS COOK & CO.
President Road
Boston

15, November 2005

To

The Post Master,

Boston City

Dear Sir,

As our daily average VPP has now reached 40, we would request you to please issue the special VP Journal.

Thanking you,

Yours faithfully,

----

11. Cancellation of an order due to non-availability of stocks.

Bookworm Publications
Ludhiana
15, December, 2005

M/s Bapuji Publications Booksellers
Mathura

Dear Sirs,

We thank you very much for your order about the supply of 100 copies of Prayers: The Path to Peace. *But we regret to say that our first edition of 11,000 books has already been exhausted, and we are not in a position to supply 100 copies to you till February 2006 when the new edition will be printed.*

In the circumstances, please treat your order as concelled. If, however, you hold on and revive this order later on, we shall certainly be glad to supply you the books.

Yours faithfully,

----

12. Insuring goods by rail.

Aftab Dry Fruits Exporters
Cochin
31, January 2005

Dear Sirs,

We shall despatch 500 cases of dry almonds by rail from Kerala to Jammu by 1804 up of 15th February.

The total value of these cases is Rs. 1,72,000.

We wish to cover the consignment from the time it leaves our godown till it reaches the godown of our clients in Jammu.

Please let us know the total amount of premium payable for insuring the goods reffered to against all risks.

Yours faithfully,

❖ ❖ ❖ ❖ ❖

4. Formal Letters — Official

Examples of Official Letters

1. **Write a letter to the Superintendent of Police of your area, complaining about some antisocial persons.**

   Govind Rao

13, Motibagh Cross,
Hussain Nagar,
Bijapur
15, July 2005

The Superintendent of Police
Lal Chowk
Bijapur

Sir,

I want to draw your immediate attention to the havoc caused by the bad social elements in our locality, Hussain Nagar. This area is haunted by many vandals. They tease young boys and girls, and drink and gamble. The move about freely with knives in their hands. Last evening they threatened a pedestrian on the main street and demanded money.

These bad characters commit all sorts of crimes. They perhaps think that no one will report against them, and the law will not punish them.

I request you to please pay a personal visit to this locality and see the things for yourself.

Yours faithfully
Abhay Verma

2. **A letter from one department to another in the government.**

GOVERNMENT OF INDIA
Cabinet Secretariat
Directorate of Public Grievances

Sardar Patel Bhawan
New Delhi – 110001
Tel: 23363733 Fax: 91-011-23345637

DPG/I/2005/0068(A)
New India Insurance Co.
Poonamalle Branch
661, Trunk Road,
Chennai – 600056

Dear Sir,

Sub: Refund of excess amount

Further to our letter under reference dated 30.5.2005.

You are hereby directed to refund an amount of Rs. 72 (Rupees Seventy two only) to Mr. A. Deendayal. It has been finally proved that your calculation of the insurance amount due from Mr. A Deendayal has not been found to be correct. In the circumstances, the insurer is entitled to a refund.

A copy of your letter addressed to Mr. Deendayal may please be endorsed to the department for information.

Thanking you,

Yours faithfully,
Sd/- BCD
(YP Yadav)
Under Secretary

3. From an individual to an organisation.

S.S. Adhikari
D-30, Sector 32,
Noida – 201303
15, April 2005

The Principal,
HIET,
16 St. Thomas Mount
Chennai – 600016

Dear Sir

Admission to Aircraft Maintenance Course

I wish to seek admission for my son, Nikunj Adhikari, on your 'Aircraft maintenance course'. Nikunj has passed his 12th class from an English medium school in New Delhi with 88% marks.

Kindly forward your prospectus along with a copy of the application. I have enclosed herewith a bank draft for Rs. 250.

Thanking you,

Yours faithfully,
SS Adhikari

4. A formal application for a job.

From

Mr. Alosius Abraham
235, Jhansi Rani Road
Vadodara

To

M/s Mothwal Bros Ltd.
23, Makkaigunj
Vadodara

Sir,

Post of Accountant

This is with reference to your advertisement in The Times of India dated 13 September 2005.

I wish to apply for the post of an Accountant in a good company. I am fairly well versed in all branches of finance. Better prospects is the purpose of this application in your company. My application therefore may please be evaluated from that angle.

If I am appointed for the post in your organisation, I assure you of my best performance to your entire satisfaction.

Thanking you,

Yours faithfully,
A. Abraham

Vadodara
14 Septemeber 2005.

5. Write an application to the Principal of your school for leave to attend your brother's wedding.

To

The Principal,
St. Mary's School,
Allahabad.

Sir,

With due respect I wish to state that my brother is getting married in Chandigarh on 10 September. Our family will be proceeding to Chandigarh on 6th. So I will be unable to attend school from 6th September to 12th September. I request you to kindly grant me leave for these days, and oblige.

Thanking you,

Yours obediently,
Naina

Dated, September 2005

6. Write an application to the Principal of your school for sick leave.

To,

The Principal,
Sacred Hearts School
Chennai.

Sir,

With due respect I beg to say that I have been suffering from high fever since yesterday evening. The doctor has advised me to take complete rest. Kindly grant me two days leave. I shall be thankful to you, sir.

Yours obediently,
Meghna Ramchandran

March 20,2005

7. Write an application to the Principal of your school for fee concession.

To

The Principal
Acharya Vidya School
Lucknow.

Sir,

With due respect I beg to say that I am a student of class 12. I am the monitor of my class and the Games Captain. My father died recently, and my mother is working in a private office as a junior clerk. We are facing financial problems at present. Hence, I request you to kindly grant me full fee concession this year and oblige.

Thanking you,

Yours obediently,
Salim Abdulla.

October 9, 2005

8. Write an application to the Principal of your school requesting him to issue you a character certificate.

To,

The Principal
Jammu Public School
Jammu.

Sir,

Respectfully I beg to state that I have passed the All India CBSC exam this year from your school. My Roll number was 2290502. I secured a high first division and was placed on the merit list.

I thank you and all the teachers who enabled me to get this distinction. I represented the school cricket team as its captain. I took active part in all the co-curricular activities. I won several prizes for debates and dramatics.

I am applying for UPSC for a competitive examination for which I need a character certificate. I request you to kindly issue me the same and oblige.

Thanking you,

Yours obediently
Thomas Jacob

20 July 2005

9. Write a letter to a newspaper complaining about poor water supply in your locality.

15, Jawahar Park Street
Kumara Park,
Mumbai,
15, July 2005

To

The Editor
Times of India
Mumbai

Sir,

I shall feel obliged if you publish the following lines in your esteemed daily in the column "Letters to the Editor".

In our colony, the water supply has been cut officially by 25 per cent. This has caused a lot of inconvenience. It is summer season and people need more water. Due to the shortage of water, many of the people have to go without a bath daily. Life has therefore become miserable. People stand in queues waiting for water. For the office-going people it has been quite strenuous. There is no other source of getting water because even the hand pumps do not work properly.

If immediate steps are not taken, it may result in breakout of diseases and epidemics, and water feminine. The authorities should take some steps for restoring the regular supply of water.

Yours faithfully

10. Write a letter to a newspaper on the recent accident at the Kumbh Mela in Haridwar.

76, Diwan's Road,
Dehradun

To

The Editor,
The Times of India,

New Delhi.

Sir,

Fifty innocent lives have been lost again due to the callousness of the administrative authorities and the VIP phobia which is obstructing the balanced growth and development of the country. In this case also, as reported in your newspaper, the tragedy occurred as a result of efforts to clear the passage for the three Chief Ministers.

VIPs are the major cause for the worries of the poor and the common man everywhere. Go the hospital anywhere, the presence of one VIP will create miseries for hundreds of patients. The VIP, even with a minor ailment will be attended to by scores of doctors with the result that the other patients are deprived of expert medical treatment and equipment. VIP roads are better maintained, and their residential colonies have better sanitation and community facilities.

If this VIP phobia is not checked immediately, ultimately the VIPs will be like kings and rulers of the past whose needs must be fulfilled at any cost.

In Haridwar, the guilty officials and politicians should be arrested immediately and charged with the murder of innocent citizens. Ordering an inquiry is a ritual. It will not give any relief to the victims. The culprits will go scot-free through political and other connections.

Yours truly

❖ ❖ ❖ ❖ ❖

PHRASES

PHRASES

Given below is a test of idiomatic phrases that are in common usage.

ABACK

To take aback: to surprise or astonish

She was clearly taken aback by his rude manner.

ABOUND

Abound with: be filled with

The pond abounds with purple lilies.

ABOUT

To go about: to set about; to try to do

She went about her work with dedication.

Beat About the Bush: indirect means to reach an object. *Beat about the bush when a simple 'Sorry' would have done?*

Out and About: do normal work.

After recuperating, he is now out and about his business.

To hang about: hover about

She hung about, hoping to have a glimpse of the matinee idol.

To come about: to happen

She hopes her dreams will come about.

To bring about: to cause or effect.

She brought about a positive change in the office atmosphere.

ACCESS

Access to: entry to

She has access to her friend's house.

ACCIDENT

By accident: by chance.

I met her by accident at the new mall.

ACCORD

To accord with: to reconcile; to grant.

She finally accorded with our plan to revamp the house.

Of one's own accord: of one's free will.

She surrendered to the police of her own accord.

ABLAZE

To set ablaze: to set fire; to burn.

The vagrants set ablaze the haystacks.

ABOVE

Above all: above everything else.

You may go out, but above all, remember to take the key.

Above board: honest.

The deal is clearly above board.

Above means: beyond income.

If you cannot afford to buy the music system, why do you want to live above means?

Above understanding: beyond one's capacity to learn.

These calculations are above my understanding.

Over and above: in addition to

Over and above her regular income, she earns a substantial sum from the savings interests.

ABSENT

Absent-minded: inattentive.

The absent-minded put his shoes in his briefcase.

ABSTAIN

Abstain from: refrain from.

The children abstained from class due to illness.

ACCEDE

Accede to: agree; give in to

He acceded to her proposal to apply for the job.

ACCOUNT

Account for: give reason for something.

We had to account for our late arrival.

Accountable to: responsible to give reason to

The workers are accountable to the supervisor.

Take into account: take into consideration.

You must take into account all the reasons given by him.

Take no account of: ignore

She took no account of his apologies.

To no account: Useless; worthless.

These papers are not signed, and hence are of no account.

ACCUSE

Accuse of: blame, bring a charge against someone

She was accused of stealing the pen.

ACID

Acid test: a severe and conclusive test.

The new job was an acid test for her.

ACQUAINT

To acquaint with: to familiarise with

She was acquainted with the workings of the office.

ACROSS

To come across: to meet with.

She came across some stiles as she neared the field.

ACT

To act upon: to act in accordance with

They acted upon the advice of their teacher

ACTION

Action-packed: full of actions

We witnessed an action-packed movie.

ADD

Add fuel to fire: increase anger; incite or rouse.

Her bitter and scathing remarks added fuel to fire at the rally.

Add insult to injury: harm or abuse

She was told to leave immediately, and the loss of pay added insult to injury.

ADEPT

Adept in: expert; skilled in.

She is adept in baking all sorts of cakes.

ADHERE

Adhere to: stick to

You must adhere to the rules of this organisation.

ADJUST

Adjust to: adapt to

All of us have to adjust to our new surroundings.

ADJACENT

Adjacent to: near to

My house is adjacent to his house.

ADVANTAGE

Have advantage over: be in a comparatively better position circumstance that gives one success.

The neatly dressed candidate has an advantage over the solvenly dressed candidate.

Take advantage of: use to one's benefit.

He took advantage of her illness to find an excuse to stay at home.

AFTER

After one's heart: according to ones choice.

This beautiful house is after my own heart.

Hanker after: seek eagerly

People are hankering after new cars these days.

AGAIN

Again and again: repeatedly.

She called him again and again.

Time and again: often

Time and again she asked my name.

Now and again: occasionally

He comes here now and again to see me.

AGAINST

Race against time: achieve before the time limit.

She was racing against time to complete the book.

AGE

To come of age: to attain adulthood.

When he comes of age he can start driving this car.

For ages: for very long time past.

It is for ages that the incident took place.

AIR

To give oneself airs: to get affected; to become proud.

Ever since you got promotion you have given yourself airs.

In the air: prevalent

I am alive to the fact that socialistic risings are in the air.

ALERT

On the alert: Watchful.

Those who were stationed were on the alert.

ALL

On all fours: to crawl on hands and knees.

I saw the robber on all fours, trying to peep inside through the window in the basement.

All in all: all-powerful

The then Prime Minister was all in all at Oxford.

All the same: nevertheless.

The boat was sailing smoothly; all the same we were afraid to move.

All there: clever; able; having quick faculties

Our friend, the judge, is all there, and knows what he is about.

All and sundry: everyone without distinction

Finally he invited all and sundry to his party

APPLE

The apple of one's eyes: much prized treasure.

This little boy's teddy is the apple of his eyes.

ARM

At arm's length: at a certain distance.

I would definitely like to keep that greedy boy at arm's length.

With open arms: warmly, affectionately

We were received at her house with open arms.

Up in arms: Ready to fight

Don't provoke them or they will be up in arms.

ASS

To make an ass of oneself: behave foolishly.

Do not make such an ass of yourself as to suppose that.

AXE

An axe to grind: a personal pecuniary interest in a matter

Our political leader has an axe to grind in standing for election in this

area.

BASE

Babes in the wood: simple, trustful children.

Though old for their age, they are still babes in the wood.

BACK

To get one's back up: become angry

His offhand manner put her back up.

To go back on a person: to betray one.

I will never go back on you, let me assure you.

To back up: to support

He prolonged the king's command, and backed him up in everything.

To back out: to refuse after consenting.

He was determined that she should not back out of the scrape so easily.

On one's back: helpless: prostrate

The doctor said that without medicines the patients would be on their backs soon.

To turn one's back upon: to desert; forsake.

The cruel man turned his back upon his wife and young children.

BAD

In bad books: out of favour with a superior.

I feel I am in my boss's bad books.

BAG

Bag and baggage: completely; leaving no property behind.

They left their house bag and baggage never to return to it again.

BARGAIN

To make the best of a bad bargain: to bear adverse circumstances in the best possible way.

They had made up their minds to submit what they could not help, and to make the best of a bad bargain.

BEAR

Bear down upon: Approach deliberately.

I saw the truck bearing down upon me.

To bear in mind: to remember

Bear in mind that you have to return the loan.

BEAT

Beat about the bush: avoid a direct statement of what must be said

Come to the point, don't beat about the bush.

To beat a retreat: to retire

Seeing the manager so grumpy, the worker beat a retreat.

BEE

In a bee line: following a straight course.

She made a bee line to the chocolate section as soon as she entered the shop.

Have a bee in one's bonnet: have a particular idea which occupies one's thought continually.

Our teacher has a bee in his bonnet about punctuation.

BEG

To go begging: be unwanted.

As no candidate was found up to the mark, the post went begging.

To beg pardon the question: to take for granted the very point of issue.

Your proposal begs the question whether a change is needed at all.

BELIEVE

To make-believe: to pretend.

Not make-believe on your part will deceive me, so tell the truth.

BELL

To bell the cat: at great personal risk, to render a common foe harmless & stet.

Now that you have spoken so well against social evils, you must also be prepared to bell the cat.

To carry the bell: to be victor in a race.

Your really must work hard for this competition if you want to carry the bell.

BELT

To hit below the belt: to strike another unfairly.

To refer to his private distresses in a public discussion was hitting below the belt.

BENT

To be bent upon: to be determined.

She was bent upon seeing this movie.

BERTH

To give a wide berth: to avoid a person

When I saw how angry my manager I was, I decided to give him a wide berth.

BEST

At the best: at the most.

At best, she can only give me a scolding.

To put one's best fot forward: to make the best show one can

At the exhibition she put her best foot forward to win the 'Best Stall' award.

To make the best of: to use to advantage.

Make the best of opportunities that come your way.

BETTER

For better or for worse: indissolubly in marriage.

The were united for better or for worse.

To get the better of: of overcome.

I soon got the better of my opponent in boxing.

BETWEEN

Between ourselves: speaking confidentially.

Let this secret be between ourselves.

BIG

To talk big: to talk boastfully.

She talks big and does nothing else.

A big-wig: a person in authority.

Sooner or later one of the big-wigs will take it up, and the point will be settled soon.

BIRD

A bird's-eye view: a general view.

The minister had a birds-eye view of the flooded area from his helicopter.

BITE

To bite the dust: to fall in battle.

That day three hundred soldiers hit the dust in the encounter with the terrorists.

BLACK

A black sheep: An disreputable member.

I am forbidden the house as I am looked upon as a black sheep.

In black and white: in writing.

Here is the confession in black and white.

To beat black and blue: to beat until the flesh is discoloured

The little kid was killed and beaten black and blue.

BLANKET

A wet blanket: one who causes others to be disheartened.

I don't want to be a wet blanket at the party.

BLOOD

In cold blood: without passion; deliberately.

The suggestion of such a plan in cold blood sent shivers down my spine.

Blue blood: aristocratic descent.

He hails from a family of blue blood.

BLOW

To blow over: to pass off.

I heard you talk of punishment but I think it has blown over.

To blow up: to lose one's temper.

She blew up when she saw the messy room.

BLUE

In the blues: melancholy.

If we had been allowed to sit idle, we should all have fallen in the blues.

A bolt from the blue: unexpected event.

The news of the solider's death was a bolt from the blue.

BLUNDER

To commit a blunder: to make a gross mistake.

While calculating the figures he committed a blunder.

BLUNT

To blunt the edge: to weaken.

The army blunted the edge of the enemy's advance by counter-attacking.

BLUSH

At the first blush: at first glance.

She was enamoured with the beauty of the sun rising at the first blush.

To put to the blush: to cause one to be ridden with shame.

Instead of putting error to the blush, she used ridicule to belittle her foe.

BOAT

To be in the same boat: To be in the same situation.

With recession setting in, the two traders found themselves in the same boat.

BODY

Body and soul: wholly; entirely.

The hard-working employee was giving his body and soul to his work.

To keep body and soul together: to sustain life.

My earnings are so miserable that they are scarcely enough to keep body and soul together.

BOLD

To make bold: to venture.

I make bold, young woman, to give you a warning about my son.

As bold as brass: impudent.

He walked in, bold as brass, and asked me to lend him Rs. 500!

BONE

A bone of contention: something which causes a quarrel.

The possession of Milan was a bone of contention between the two monarchs.

To make no bones: publish openly.

He makes no bones of his dislike of natives.

BOOK

In the good books of: in favour with.

I was so much in his good books that at his death he left me a substantial sum of money.

To bring to book: to call to account.

He was caught cheating and was brought to book by the examiner.

BORN

Not born yesterday: worldly-wise.

She may look young, but she can see as far ahead as most others, for she wasn't born yesterday.

BOSOM

A bosom friend: a very intimate friend.

I share my secrets with my bosom friend.

BOTTOM

To be at the bottom of: to be the real cause of.

He is a trouble-maker and is at the bottom of the whole rift in the office.

BOUND

Out of bounds: prohibited.

The forest is out of bounds for the school children.

BOW

To bow to: submit.

She had to bow to pressure to change her plans.

BOWL

To bowl over: to knock down.

Very soon their last defence was bowled over.

BOX

To be in a box: to be in a fix.

He was in a box trying to choose the best option for the deal.

BREAD

To break bread: to eat; be a guest.

He was invited to break bread at the royal house.

Bread and butter: material welfare, livelihood.

The old man worked hard for his bread and butter.

BREAK

To break down: to lose control over one's feelings.

On seeing her son hospitalised, she broke down.

To break off: to renounce the acquaintance of.

She consented to break off with him.

To break the ice: to commence a conversation where there has been an awkward silence.

As there was pin-drop silence, he decided to break the ice.

To break the news: to impart starting news.

He broke the news to her about his expulsion from the factory.

BREAST

To make a clean breast of: to make a full and clean confession of something.

She resolved to make a clean breast of the whole affair.

BREATH

Under one's breath: very quietly.

She spoke under her breath about her plans of eloping.

With bated breath: to be restrained because of reverence or fear:

She waited with bated breath to hear the results of the competition.

BREATHE

To breathe one's last: To die.

The injured man breathed his last without gaining consciousness.

BRING

To bring round: to restore.

Do you think you could bring the unconscious man round?

To bring about: to cause to happen.

We are confident of bringing about the much needed alliance with Iran.

To bring to mind: to recollect.

You must bring to mind what happened next.

To bring under: to subdue.

The clashes were brought under by the timely action of the police.

To bring to light: to disclose.

The lawyer brought to light many interesting facts.

To bring home: to impress; to prove.

The teacher brought home the advantages of punctuality to his students.

BUCKLE

To buckle to: to work zealously.

We all buckled to with a will, doing ten hours a day.

BUD

To nip in the bud: to destroy at an early stage

Guessing his intentions, she resolved to nip them in the bud.

BULL

To hit the bull's eye: to score a great success.

The Republicans hit the bull's eye, and were jubilant.

To take the bull by the horns: to attack something in a bold and direct fashion.

Seeing lethargy all round him, he decided to take the bull by the horns, and punish the lazy ones.

BURN

To burn one's fingers: to suffer loss or hurt by meddling unnecessarily.

It would be wise to keep away from his affairs, or else you will burn your fingers.

To burn one's boats: to leave no means of retreat.

Think before resigning; if you do resign you would have burnt your boats.

BURY

To bury the hatchet: to cease fighting.

Both nations, in their efforts towards reconciliation and peace, have buried the hatchet.

BUSINESS

To mean business: to be in earnest.

When the lender comes to you, he means business.

BY

By the by: in passing.

By the by, did you notice that signboard over the building?

By book or by crook: by fair or foul means.

He always wins the deal by hook or by crook.

CAKE

To take the cake: to be first in a contest.

The Wesleyans take the cake, having by far the finest church building in their city.

CALL

To call names: to speak disrespectfully of a person.

He was punished for calling his teacher names.

To call upon: to invoke the aid of.

I now call upon the chairman to address the meeting.

To call in question: To challenge or throw doubt upon.

He is a clean person, and it is undesirable to call his honesty in question.

CAPITAL

To make capital out of: to use anything for one's own profit.

He made capital of their recently signed deal.

CARD

On the cards: probable.

The game going to the Aussies is very much on the cards.

To throw up one's cards: to cease to struggle.

He saw at once that his employer was right, and that it only remained for him to throw up his cards.

CARRY

To carry the day: to prove superior, to win.

When such discussions arise, money generally carries the day.

To carry out: to execute.

To carry out the aims he had in view, he made use of persons he trusted.

To carry one's point: to succeed in one's aim.

They were bent on placing him in the Speaker's chair, and they carried their point triumphantly.

CAST

To cast about: to search mentally or physically.

He cast about for a comfortable seat.

To cast down: to be low in spirits.

For my part I was horribly cast down by the news of his death.

CAT

To let the cat out of the bag: to disclose a secret.

By revealing their plans he let the cat out of the bag.

A cat and dog life: a life of petty quarrels.

The newly wedded couple were soon leading a cat-and-dog life.

To rain cats and dogs: to rain heavily

When we stepped out, to our dismay it started raining cats and dogs.

To make a cat's paw of: to use as a mere tool.

She has made a cat's paw of you, that's sure.

To grin like a cheshire cat: to be always smiling with the teeth displayed.

On seeing his new toy he grinned like a Cheshire cat.

CATCH

To catch up: to overtake.

He was ill for a long time, and now he has to catch up with the others in his studies.

CAUSE

To make common cause with: to side with and support.

Everyone has to make it a common cause for the programme to work out well.

CAVE

To cave in: to succumb.

He was very adamant at first, but caved in under pressure.

CHAIR

To take the chair: to preside.

He was asked to take the chair and steer the seminar.

CHILD

Child's play: something very easy.

It is child's play for a magician to pull a rabbit out of a hat.

CLEAR

To clear out: to empty.

I think you have to clear out all the unwanted items from your cupboard.

CLOUD

To be under a cloud: to be in disgrace.

Her reputation is under a cloud because she was seen with a boy at midnight.

COAT

To turn one's coat: to change to the opposite party.

This is not the first time he has changed coat.

COCK

A cock-and-bull story: an absurd tale.

Don't expect me to believe such a cock-and-bull story.

COIN

To pay a man back in his own coin: to serve him as he has served you.

Unless paid back in his own coin, he will not stop telling lies.

COME

To come about: to happen.

This has come about because of your carelessness.

To come across: to meet.

I came across my friend at the shop.

To come to light: to become known.

Soon her deceptive ways came to light.

To come to a standstill: to stop

On seeing the strange man, all work came to a standstill.

To come to grief: to be unsuccessful.

The Panama Canal scheme is likely to come to grief owing to want of funds.

To come to pass: to happen.

What you predicted has come to pass.

To come to the point: to speak plainly and directly.

After a lot of explanations, he finally came to the point.

COMMIT

To commit to memory: to learn by heart.

When young, he committed to memory the whole of the psalms.

COMMON

In common: held equally with others.

Poor people, who have their goods in common, must necessarily become quarralsome.

CONSCIENCE

In all conscience: assuredly.

Plain and precise enough it is, in all conscience.

COUNT

To count upon: to trust to.

I count upon you to find the solution to this puzzle.

COURSE

In course: in regular order.

You will receive the other journals in course.

In due course: at the proper time.

I shall tell you the results in due course.

CROP

To crop out: to appear above the surface.

The prejudice of the editor crops out in his writings.

To crop up: to appear unexpectedly.

But soon complications were to crop up.

CROW

As the crow flies: directly

He went, as the crow flies, over the fields till he reached the gate.

To crow over: to triumph over

She won the race and won't stop crowing over.

CRY

To cry over spilt milk: to spend time in useless regrets.

What's done cannot be helped; so don't cry over spilt milk.

CUDGELS

To take up cudgels: to engage in a contest *when dared, he took up cudgels, and proved his courage.*

CUT

To cut one short: to interrupt another while speaking.

He started speaking scathingly, but I cut him short.

To be cut up: to be distressed.

He was awfully cut up at having to leave you alone.

To cut and run: to go off quickly.

I must cut and run, whatever happens.

DAGGERS

To look daggers at: to glare at.

Knowing she was telling a tie, I looked daggers at her.

DARK

To keep one in the dark: to keep one in ignorance.

Since I didn't want to hurt her feelings, I kept her in the dark about her husband's affairs.

DEAD

Dead as a doornail: stone dead.

She lay there, dead as a doornail.

A dead letter: a rule never attended to.

The rule about ready money was soon a dead letter

Dead beat: thoroughly exhausted

He sat down dead beat after the marathon race.

DEATH

At death's door: very near dying.

The old man confessed to the priest at death's door.

DEVIL

Devils luck: good fortune.

You always have the devil's luck in bargains

DIRT

Dirt cheap: at an excessively low price.

These second-hand goods are dirt cheap.

DOG

A dog-in-the manger: a selfish man.

He had a dog-in-the-manger course of conduct.

To go to the dogs: to go to ruin.

His house had been neglected, and so has gone to the dogs.

To lead a dog's life: to pass a miserable existence.

I am afraid I led that boy a dog's life.

DRAW

To draw the line: to impose an arbitrary restriction on one's behaviour.

You can watch the television but I draw the line when it comes to going out with your friend at night.

DROP

To drop in: to pay an informal visit.

If you can drop in tomorrow, I shall hand over the papers to you.

DUST

To raise a dust: to make a commotion.

There was no need to raise a dust over such a small matter.

EAR

To give ear: to listen.

I wish you will give ear to my poem.

EASE

Ill at ease: restless.

He is ill at ease when he sees blind people.

EAT

To eat one's words: to take back what was said.

I now know I am in the wrong, and I eat my words.

EGG

To have all one's eggs in one basket: to risk all one's goods in the same venture.

I know your happiness depends on her, as all your eggs are in that one basket.

ELBOW

Elbow room: sufficient space.

Your must have elbow room here; so remove the unnecessary furniture from here.

END

To make both ends meet: to keep out of debt.

They are a poor family, who find it difficult to both ends meet.

EYE

See eye to eye: have the same opinions about something.

Until we see eye to eye on the question, let us stay apart.

FACE

A long face: a sad or mournful expression.

When she realised how badly she had fared in the exams, she wore a long face.

Face to face: facing directly each other in front of.

They had a face to face talk about the matter of their marriage.

To put a bold face upon: to act boldly.

He had nothing to prove his innocence, but be put a hold face upon the matter.

FAIR

Fair game: deserving of barter or criticism.

John is fair game, but all of his statements are not worthless.

Fair and square: honest; just.

He signed the deal which was fair and square.

Fair play: just treatment.

The judges of the beauty contest believed in fair play.

FAITH

In good faith: without treachery.

We all believe that he had acted in good faith.

FALL

To fall flat: cause no amusement.

His remarks fell flat at the party.

To fall out: to quarrel.

They fell out over the issue of payment of wages.

FAR

A far cry: a long distance.

It is a far cry from Paris to Tokyo.

Far from it: by no means.

I imagined him to be handsome, but he was far from being so.

FAST

To play fast and loose: have no consideration for.

It's a shame to play fast and loose with a young girl's affections.

FAT

To kill the fatted calf: to prepare the best food in the house for an expected guest.

They killed the fatted calf when the newly weds arrived at their place for dinner.

FAULT

To find fault with: to blame.

She always loves to find fault with her juniors.

FEATHER

A feather in one's cap: an honour.

He won the Oscar Award as well, and that is a feather in his cap.

FIDDLE

To play second fiddle: to take a subordinate role.

She always plays second fiddle to him in dramas.

FINGER

A finger in the pie: He mixed up in something.

He has a finger in every pie, and feels proud about it.

FISH

A fish out of water: A person in uneasy situations.

I felt a fish out of water at the party.

A queer fish: an eccentric person.

He is such a queer fish that people avoid him.

To fish for compliments: try to gain by indirect methods.

I know you are fishing for compliments about your book.

Other fish to fry: Other business to attend to.

Besides escorting his children to school, he has other fish to fry.

FITS

By fits and starts: spasmodically.

By working in fits and starts you will not progress.

FLASH

A flash in the pan: an abortive attempt.

His first novel was a flash in the pan, and he has not written since.

FLEA

A flea in one's ear: an unwelcome repulse for his derogatory remarks.

He was sent out with a flea in his ear.

FLESH

Flesh and blood: human nature.

It was more than flesh and blood could bear.

To make the flesh creep: to cause dread and horror.

You make my flesh creep with your horror stories.

FLY

With flying colours: honourably.

She came out with plying colours at the interview.

FOOL

A fool's paradise: a state of happiness that is unreal.

Get out of living in a fool's paradise.

FOOT

With one foot in the grave: very feeble, with short time to live.

With one foot in the grave, he can hardly manage the factory.

FORTY

Forty winks: a snooze.

She had forty winks before resuming her work.

GAUNTLET

To throw the gauntlet: to challenge.

The company threw the gauntlet to all the sailors in the world.

GIVE

To give in: to concede.

They did not give in till they were depleted of all their men.

GOOD

For good: completely.

She has gone away for good from here.

GRASS

Let the grass grow under one's feet: be idle.

Be more active and don't let the grass grow under your feet.

GREEN

The green-eyed monster: jealousy

She was green with jealousy but tried to hide under pretensions of admiration.

GROUND

To hold one's ground: to be firm.

He made a supreme effort to hold his ground.

GUARD

Off one's guard: heedless; forgetful; in a carelass state.

He caught both men off their guard.

HAMMER

Hammer and tongs: act violently and recklessly when the match began.

Both teams went to it hammer and tongs.

HAND

An old hand: an experienced man.

He is an old hand at handling delicate situations.

HANG

To hang fire: to delay the accomplishment or come to no decisive result

The plan began to hang fire.

HARD

Hard and fast: securely.

I have got the thief hard and fast.

HARE

As mad as a march hare: crazy.

The old man is as mad as a march hare to make such stupid suggestions.

HAT

To pass round the hat: to solicit subscriptions.

At the charity fare he passed round the hat.

HAUL

To haul over the coals: to administer rebuke.

This is no way of hauling me over the coals for being idle.

HAVE

To have it out: to settle a disputed point.

I was inclined to have it out with him for his lack of consideration.

HEAD

To make neither head nor tail of anything: to be unable to understand of something.

You said something queer and I could make neither head nor tail of it.

Head and shoulders: by the height of the head and shoulders.

My son is head and shoulders taller than mother.

HEART

To wear one's heart upon one's sleeve: to expose one's inmost thoughts to all.

You could make out that she was in love as she wore her heart upon her sleeve.

To break one's heart: to be mortally disappointed.

It broke her heart to see him so frail and weak.

Heart and soul: enthusiastically

He went into the scheme heart and soul.

To have one's heart in one's mouth: to be frightened or startled.

He had his heart in his mouth when he went for a medical examination.

HEELS

To take to one's heels: to run off

On seeing policemen, the robbers took to their heels.

HORSE

To ride the high horse: to have a haughty manner.

As the manager of the club he rides the high horse.

HIT

To hit the nail on the head: to touch the exact point.

She hit the nail on the head when she said that the maid had stolen the purse.

HITHER

Hither and thither: in various directions.

The crowd ran hither and thither on seeing the policemen with teargas shells.

HOME

To make our self at home: to act as if one were in one's own home.

The thieves entered the house and made themselves at home when no one was in.

HOUR

At the eleventh hour: just in time.

She handed over the examination sheets at the eleventh hour.

HOUSE

Like a house on fire: very rapidly and easily.

The friends got on like a house on fire.

HUE

Hue and cry: a clamour in pursuit of an offender.

A hue and cry followed in the wake of the robbery.

HUMBLE

To eat humble pie: to apologise abjectly.

The tyrant is making France eat humble pie.

JACK

A jack of all trades: a man who has many occupations.

My brother is a jack of all trades, and carries out all the repairs by himself.

KICK

To kick the bucket: to die.

The old man soon kicked the bucket.

KITH

Kith and kin: relatives.

He loves his friends more than his kith and kin.

LAUGH

To laugh in one's sleeve: to smile inwardly while preserving a serious face.

How they must have laughed in their sleeve when they saw you falll flat on your nose.

LEAF

To turn over a new leaf: to begin a different mode of life.

Now that he has recovered from the tragedy, I hope he will turn over a new leaf.

LEAP

By leaps and bounds: quickly.

She progressed in her career by leaps and bounds.

LEG

On its last legs: about to perish.

The poor dog is on its last legs.

LION

The lion's share: a disproportionately large share.

The eldest son took the lion's share of the wealth.

LONG

In the long run: eventually.

In the long run, the money deposit will yield good returns.

LOOK

To look through coloured spectacles: to see things not as they really are, but affected by own prejudices.

People who live much by themselves are apt to look at things through coloured spectacles.

LURCH

To leave in the lunch: to abandon.

You are so mean that if he leaves you in the lurch it would serve you right.

MAKE

To make believe: to pretend.

We have to make believe that we have won it all.

To make up for: to compensate for.

She is working hard to make up for her husband's repeated absences.

MOUNTAIN

To make a mountain of a molehill: to magnify a simple matter.

Stuff and nonsense! You are making a mountain out of a molehill, as you always do.

MOUTH

By word of mouth: verbally.

The message was given by word of mouth, not written.

MOVE

To move heaven and earth: to make every possible effort.

We shall move heaven and earth to get him out of this mess.

MUD

To throw mud at: to abuse.

A woman in my position must expect to have more mud thrown at her than a less important person.

NEST

Feather one's next: to provide for one's future.

Since he has feathered his next, he can afford to lose a little business.

NOSE

To pay through the nose: to pay a large sum

Instead of making a fuss, I paid him through the nose everything that he claimed.

NOW

Now and then: at intervals.

He visits me now and then.

NULL

Null and void: of no effect.

This document has no name and hence is null and void.

NUT

A hard nut to crack: a difficult problem to solve.

He found that particular poser a hard nut to crack.

NUTSHELL

In a nutshell: simply and briefly.

You have described the events very well in a nutshell.

OAR

To rest on ones oar's: to cease from hard work.

After finishing my education I went home for a brief stay to rest on my oars.

OATS

To sow one's wild oats: to indulge in youthful excesses.

His taste for betting might turn out to be something more than sowing wild oats.

ODDS

Odds and ends: stray articles.

He picked up odds and ends at the sales.

OFF

Off and on: at intervals.

She visits me off and on.

OIL

To pour oil on troubled waters: to act as peacemaker.

Iustead of making matters worse, try to pour oil on troubled waters to pacify them.

OINTMENT

A fly in the ointment: that which spoils the excellence of something.

The deal was good except for a clause which acted as a fly in the ointment.

OLIVE

To hold out the olive branch: to call for a truce.

His sudden appearance, holding out the olive branch, was unexpected.

ONCE

Once and for all: finally.

I must tell you once and for all that you will get nothing by kneeling to me.

Once in a way: occasionally.

He comes home once in a way.

OPEN

An open secret: a piece of news not formally declared, yet known to all.

It was an open secret that he would be appointed as the governor.

OUT

Out and out: thoroughly.

She was out and out a noble person with a kind and generous disposition.

OVER

Over and above: in addition.

I have to pay Rs. 500 over and above the cost of this toaster.

PART

Part and parcel: an essential part.

She is part and parcel of our family.

PICK

To pick a bone with one: to find fault with one.

She had a bone to pick with her husband as he had forgotten to wish her on her birthday.

PIECE

To give someone a piece of one's mind: to tell him unpleasant truths.

She gave her son a piece of her mind as he had not finished his homework.

PILLAR

From pillar to post: hither and thither.

She went campaigning and asking for donations from pillar to post.

PLAIN

Plain as a pikestaff: very plain and evident.

He is not interested in it and has made his view plain as a pikestaff.

PLAY

To play truant: to absent oneself without leave.

The child decided to play truant and skip going to school that day.

PLUCK

To pluck up courage: to throw fear aside.

The child plucked up courage and showed his progress card to his father.

POINT

Point blank: directly.

She refused you point blank, I guess.

POKE

To poke fun at: to ridicule.

Seeing him grin, I thought he was poking fun at me.

POLISH

To polish off: to finish.

The dog polished off all the food from its plate.

POOR

Poor as a church mouse: very poor.

Our servant is poor as a church mouse.

PRO

Pros and cons: minute discussion.

After a few pros and cons they decided to end the matter there forever.

PUT

To put two and two together: to reason.

When she saw everyone sitting glumly, she put two and two together and realised they had quarrelled.

QUESTION

A burning question: a subject of widespread interest.

People like to read about a burning question when they are at leisure.

RACK

To go to rack and ruin: to fall into utter disrepair.

That house has surely gone to rack and ruin by now.

RANK

The rank and file: the undistinguished mass.

The rank and file of his parliamentary opponents sought to laugh him down.

REAR

To bring up the rear: to come last.

The rear of the file was brought up by two soldiers.

RECKON

To reckon with: to settle accounts with.

You will have to reckon with your landlord.

RED

A redletter day: an auspicious or happy day.

When I won the award for being the best student in school it was a red-letter day for me.

RESPECT

To pay one's respects: to make one a polite visit.

She went there every day to pay her respects to the kind, old lady.

RHYME

Without rhyme for reason: no sense or logic.

She left the place suddenly without rhyme or reason.

ROSE

A bed of roses: a very comfortable situation.

Life could not have been a bed of roses for any of them.

SALT

Worth one's salt: of value.

Every man who is worth his salt has his enemies.

SCARCE

To make oneself scarce: to retire; to withdraw.

Whenever he comes home, she makes herself scarce.

SCOT

Scot free: quite uninjured.

The accused got off scot free as there was not evidence against him.

SEA

At sea: in a state of perplexity.

She tried to understand the instructions, but she was completely at sea.

SERVE

To serve one's turn: to be useful on occasion.

His connection with the press serves our turn.

SET

To set on foot: to start.

He was asked to set the scheme on foot.

To set sail: to start on a voyage.

The family set soil in a cruise ship bound for the Mediterranean.

SEVEN

A seven days' wonder: something of interest for a while and then forgotten.

The seven days' wonder about the boy had almost died down.

SHAKE

To shake in one's shoes: to be in nervous terror.

Whenever he spoke of the fire, she shook in her shoes.

SHOP

To talk shop: to talk only of one's business.

She did not like his talking shop during parties.

SHORT

A short cut: a quick path.

She took a short cut to school.

SHOULDER

To give one the cold shoulder: to treat coolly.

Since I accused him of lying, he has turned the cold shoulder upon me.

SHOW

To show off: to make a vain display.

She tried to show off her expensive jewellery.

SIGHT

Out of sight: not in sight.

She turned the corner and was soon out of sight.

A sight for sore eyes: something pleasant to see.

Her ever-smiling face is a sight for sore eyes.

SKIN

To escape by the skin of one's teeth: to escape very narrowly.

He escaped the accident only by the skin of his teeth.

To save one's skin: to get off without bodily hurt.

He jumped aside to save his skin as the car flashed past him.

SKIP

To skip over: to pass unnoticed.

She decided to skip over the details and just narrate the bare outline.

SLIP

To give the slip: to escape secretly.

He was following me and I was wondering how to give him the slip when you appeared.

To slip through one's fingers: to escape from one's grasp.

The little rascal shpped through their fingurs.

SLOW

A slow coach: a lazy or inactive person.

He is not quick in anything, and so we call him a slow coach.

SMELL

To smell a rat: to detect something wrong.

He will smell a rat if you suddenly volunteer to help him.

SOUR

Sour grapes: a thing despised because it is unattainable.

He said that he didn't want to marry her anyway, but that's just sour grapes.

SOW

To sow wild oats: to be wild and extravagant in youth.

He sowed all his oats before he married.

SPADE

To call a spade a spade: to use plain language.

She doesn't mince words and calls a spade a spade

SPICK

Spick and span: very neat and trim.

There was a spic and span loy stauding at the door.

SPIN

To spin a yarn: to tell a story.

Whenever he came home late, he always indulged in spinning a yarn.

SPLIT

To split hairs: to indulge in refined arguments.

Though the case was simple, the lawyer wanted to split hairs.

SPOKE

To put a spoke in someone's wheel: to arrest his progress.

You have put a formidable spoke in my wheel by preventing the extension of my tenure at the office.

SPUR

On the spur of the moment: without rejection.

The criticism was offered on the spur of the moment.

SQUARE

A square meal: a full meal that satisfies.

Even at the age of eight he ate but one square meal a day.

STEAL

To steel a march upon: to gain an advantage over an enemy without knowing it.

One day he woke up early and stole a march on his nurses by walking out of the hospital.

STONE

Stone blind: completely blind.

He cannot see as he is stone blind.

A stone's throw: very near.

His house is a stone's throw from our shop.

To leave no stone unturned: to take all possible means towards gaining something.

I will leave no stone unturned with the lawyer regarding your case.

TABLE

To turn the tables: to reverse the position of two rival parties.

He was winning, but soon his opponent took the lead, turning the tables.

TAIL

To turn tail: to retreated in an undignified way.

When he saw himself on the battlefield, he turned tail and fled.

TAKE

To take after: to resemble.

The girl takes after her father.

To take by storm: to secure by one great effort.

The lovely girl with her sweet speech took the men's hearts by storm.

To take to one's heels: to commence running.

On seeing the approaching policeman, he took to his heels.

To take to task: to reprove.

She was taken to task for neglecting her work.

TEA

A storm in a teacup: a petty squabble.

It is nothing serious to worry about; it's just a storm in a teacup.

TENTERHOOKS

On tenterhooks: in a state of discomfort forgoing.

I should like to have it settled as soon as possible because it keeps a man on tenterhooks.

THICK

Through thick and thin: through every obstacle.

He stood by me through thick and thin when my wife died.

Thick-skinned: not sensitive.

You need a thick skin to be a politician.

TIDE

To tide over: to overcome a difficulty temporarily.

This amount is enough for him to tide over for the present.

TIME

In no time: very quickly.

In no time she finished painting the scenery.

From time to time: at intervals

She lived with them, only visiting her grandmother from time to time.

TIT

Tit for tat: just retaliation.

He hit me and I hit him back – it was tit for tat.

TO

To and fro: backwards and forwards.

The spiders swing idly to and fro from their webs.

TOOTH

Tooth and nail: with great energy.

The children fought tooth and nail for that loaf of bread.

TREAD

To tread on someone's toes: to annoy someone.

I won't tread on your toes and so will keep silent about that affair.

TRUMPET

To blow one's own teumpet: to speak boastfully

After such a victory he is now blowing his own teumpet.

TURN

To turn a deaf ear: to refuse to listen.

The government has turned a deaf ear to the requests made for new legislations.

UP

Up and about: no longer in bed.

By the time he woke up, she was already up and about.

Up in arms: ready to quarrel..

He would have been up in arns, no doubt, if he had known it.

Ups and downs: successives rises and falls.

The ups and downs of the ruling party furnished subjects for excellent cartoons.

Up to something: about to carry out a scheme.

His furtive movements suggest that he is up to something.

VOLUMES

To speak volumes: to be very significant.

His hesitant manner spoke volumes about his involvement in the scam.

WATER

In deep water: in difficulties.

I know he is in deep water after losing his passport.

WAY

Once in a way: occasionally.

Once in a way he may drink too much.

To give way: to yield or submit.

I have never seen the bridegroom's male friends give way to tears.

WEAR

Wear and tear: damage resulting from constant use.

The castle walls have stood the wear and tear of centuries.

WHITE

A white lie: a statement that is verbally true, but really and essentially false.

She would rather tell a white lie than hurt her father's feelings.

White as a sheet: intensely pale.

On hearing a terrible crash, he turned white as a sheet.

A white elephant: a useless possession that is often expensive to maintain.

We are moving into a smaller house as this very large house is a white elephant.

WIDE

Wide awake: alert.

He is wide awake to the needs of his business.

WILD

A wild goose chase: a foolish and fruitless search.

The hoaxer had sent the police on a wild goose chase.

WIND

To take the wind out of someone's sails: to gain a clever advantage over another.

Being beaten by a newcomer has really taken the wind out of his sails.

To get wind of: to learn about.

I could get wind of the amount he gaver to charity if I wanted.

To take under one's wing: to protect.

We heard you were under Mary's care, and that you felt safe.

To lend wings to: to hasten.

The sound of bricks falling behind them lent them wings.

WIT

At wit's end: wholly puzzled how to act.

He was almost at his wit's end how to calm the sobbing lady.

WOOL

Pull the wool over one's eyes: to cheat.

It is no use trying to pull over his eyes as he is too smart for it.

WORTH

Worth one's salt: efficient; a good workman.

It was plain from every line of his body that our new hand was worth his salt.

❖ ❖ ❖ ❖ ❖